FREE MAN
AND THE CORPORATION

McKINSEY FOUNDATION LECTURE SERIES

Sponsored by the
Graduate School of Business, Columbia University

Blough—*Free Man and the Corporation*

Cordiner—*New Frontiers for Professional Managers*

Greenewalt—*The Uncommon Man*

Houser—*Big Business and Human Values*

FREE MAN
AND THE CORPORATION

ROGER M. BLOUGH
Chairman, United States Steel Corporation

McGraw-Hill Book Company, Inc.
NEW YORK   TORONTO   LONDON   1959

PREFACE

In these times of international tension and struggle between the proponents of a free democratic way of life and those of the totalitarian, state-oriented systems, we in the United States too often have taken for granted the economic, social, and spiritual freedom, and the material abundance we enjoy. We have failed to question as fully as we should just what there is about our system that makes both freedom and growth possible. As a result, we find all too frequently prescriptions for economic and political ends that bear resemblance to the patterns of the authoritarians with whom we are in contest.

In 1955 the McKinsey Foundation for Management Research, Inc., made an initial grant to the Graduate School of Business of Columbia University designed to encourage a series of lectures

v

leading to a better understanding of the management of large organizations in our complex society. It was hoped that the School could find among the leaders of the business community those who combine the attributes which make them successful men of action, with the perspective and philosophical depth to describe the essential nature of our business system and its relationships with other parts of our social order.

The first three McKinsey lecturers, Mr. Ralph J. Cordiner, President of General Electric Company, Mr. Theodore V. Houser, Chairman of the Board of Sears, Roebuck and Co., and Mr. Crawford H. Greenewalt, President of E. I. du Pont de Nemours & Company, Inc., addressed themselves to different aspects of this vital subject. The published volumes of their lectures, titled *New Frontiers for Professional Managers*, *Big Business and Human Values*, and *The Uncommon Man*, respectively, have had wide circulation, including in instances French, German, and Japanese translations. The School was fortunate in adding to this distinguished group the man who authors this year's lectures.

Mr. Roger M. Blough, Chairman of the Board of The United States Steel Corporation, serves as the chief executive officer of the leading company in one of America's pivotal industries. He made full use of his rich business experience and intellectual abilities as he described in these lectures the essential nature of the corporation and its role in our free way of life.

To Mr. Blough, the foundation of our free society is our deep-seated belief in the inherent rights and capabilities of the individual. Among these rights is the right voluntarily to associate or disassociate to accomplish legitimate purposes. It is the genius of the American people that they have found the means to collaborate voluntarily for so many group objectives, including the provision of abundance. From this premise rises the framework of free initiative and our present corporate system. He feels that only when we as a people grow to understand more fully this essential nature of our business system can we appreciate the implications of our actions as workers, consumers, managers, and voters.

The lectures begin by defining a modern corporation, not in legalistic or functional terms, but rather as people—people coming together freely, seeking the corporation as a way of realizing their individual and group aspirations. With insight and depth of understanding, the author discusses the nature of this voluntary association and presents it as one expression of the great strength of our spiritual freedom. He points out that individuals, though free to pursue only individual ends to the extent of their ability, modify in varying degrees the pursuit of individual goals in recognition of the rights and interests of others with whom they are in association. This is done in our society not by edict, nor by a national super ego attempting to act as a conscience for all, but by laws and social mores created by the mutual consent of those who are prepared to abide by them.

After exploring the nature of this voluntary association of individuals who have formed a corporate group, Mr. Blough moves to a discussion of the relationship between this group and other groups to which these same individuals may belong. He specifically considers the relationship between the corporate group, government, and union groups. He is especially interested in the responsibilities of each group to its members and to the members of the other groups with which they are in close and continuing contact. The question is raised whether some labor groups may not have let their internal interests override the broader interests of society.

In this thoughtful analysis of the American business system by one of its leaders, the reader may be assured of gaining insights into the nature of free enterprise or, in alternative words—the nature of *voluntary progress*. His interests range from such diverse subjects as the support of nonprofit organizations to the development of management tools in a democratically administered business organization.

With the assistance of Mr. Howard C. Johnson of The United States Steel Corporation and Mr. E. Kirby Warren of the Columbia Graduate School of Business, Mr. Blough has added to the original text portions of the discussions between himself and the business and academic leaders who attended the dinners which followed each lecture. These additions provide still further illumination of the nature of the subject discussed so thoughtfully in the lecture series.

COURTNEY C. BROWN
Dean, Graduate School of Business
Columbia University

A WORD ABOUT PURPOSE

The broad charter of the McKinsey Lectures seeks to widen our knowledge and understanding of enterprise in America—to examine its place in our society, its contributions, its strength, and its vulnerability.

This charter of purpose thus seeks, as I comprehend it, to examine how men in a free society enhance their talents, voluntarily and creatively, through corporate effort. And this poses a task of no small dimensions.

If my response to this broad inquiry is less than full illumination, the reader should not be surprised. For it is not easy to find the answers to many of the perplexing questions which confront us as we contemplate the modern corporation and its works. However objectively one may wish to approach the task, however deep the belief in the value of what we are doing, it is all too easy to misinterpret, overstate, or fail to see ourselves as others see us. And for this I bespeak the reader's indulgence.

Many no doubt will see the corporation as I do—voluntary man's way of achieving industrial competence—as the master key to material growth in a greater society. Others, conversely, will see it as a fearsome thing which is multiplying apace, in size and in numbers. With uneasy foreboding, they envision the possibility of group conflict and they have searched for countervailing power or greater direction by government—forgetting perhaps that size is not power and that usefulness is not evil.

I suppose, too, that, to many, a corporation is a legalistic thing, a certificate to organize in pursuit of a stated objective. To others it may be a materialistic aggregation of tools, machines, and other capital facilities necessary to production.

But to those of us who work with it, live with it, suffer with it, and achieve with it, a corporation, in a very realistic sense, is people—a voluntary productive group composed of real, live individuals—not automatons. Perceiving this, I believe, is the gateway to understanding this useful instrumentality.

CONTENTS

Preface   v

A Word about Purpose   xi

Voluntary Man—His Way to Economic Growth   1

Creative Man—His Work and the Union   41

Citizen Man—His Group and His Government   81

VOLUNTARY MAN—
HIS WAY TO
ECONOMIC GROWTH

PRODUCTIVE GROUPS IN
A FREE SOCIETY

In exploring the way of voluntary man to economic growth in a free society, let us pause briefly to observe that a "free" society—as the term is used here—is not a synonym for a "free and easy" society. A more apt description would be a "free, responsible, and responsive society"—one in which individuals, bonded together as a nation, are at once possessed of freedom of choice, a personal sense of respect for the rights of their fellows, and an abhorrence of compulsion in mutual affairs—a society in which individuals are responsive to the changing boundaries of thought, of culture, and of conscience. In a free society each person not only has a set of values but also has the capacity fearlessly to make and remake judgments regarding those values, and the freedom to act on those judgments.

But it is not my purpose to present the case for a free society. I presume that we may gratefully postulate a free society, not only as a goal but with the deepest conviction that only in a free society can man's dignity as a person be maintained and only there may he attain the destiny for which, as all of us instinctively know and our religions proclaim, he was created.

We may not and do not forget that the majority of men now live in a world of compulsion and that both a society of compulsion and a free society are capable of increasing a nation's material strength, although I believe a free society will do it more adequately, and that either the voluntary or the compulsory society will produce men of resolute purpose.

But for us the clear choice is a free society—not for any productive or material advantages it may enjoy but because of our deep-seated belief that wherever and to whatever extent compulsion is needlessly substituted for choice, to that extent people are less free and the opportunities of mankind are diminished.

Now it is a notable characteristic of a free society that men will voluntarily join forces for their common welfare—material or spiritual—and that, of the many ways to improve human welfare, by all odds

4

the voluntary route of group cooperation of like-minded individuals has proved to be the most effective. The newly founded family, when observed from one point of view, is a cohesive economic group. The church is a voluntary group activity for the fulfillment of spiritual aspirations. A great university, like Columbia, is another example of voluntary cooperation. The list is endless—men voluntarily joining together for their common protection, their common improvement, or their common enjoyment.

This freedom for individuals to form associations and to join or not to join is an important "freedom" in our society, elementary but basic, and only when we accept it as basic and completely understand it can we examine fruitfully the free institutions in a free society, of which the group organized for production—and for convenience called a corporation— is a vital example.

I do not, by any means, intend to imply that this underlying concept of freedom of individuals to join with others solves all or any of the questions which relate to corporations. But I do believe this concept will help us to think about these questions and help us arrive at reasonable conclusions. In that way, we shall start, as it were, with a common premise, however broad it may be.

Now let us consider one other rather basic point at the beginning. Our physical world is what it is, a world of increasingly powerful and complex physical things—a world, for example, of atomic fission and fusion, of transmission of sound and of images, even in color, of a continuous flow of information and of mass media, of giant machines in mill and factory, of great transportation systems—altogether a physical world astonishing in its changing complexion, filling man's wants and his wonder as it now expands into space and comprehends particles of imperceptible size.

And central to our thought is this readily acceptable point. The essential purposes which man wants to, can, and must accomplish, such as those just mentioned, can only be achieved in our free society if men cooperate in the doing—cooperate by forming groups of individuals who undertake dissimilar parts of the work and who, by working together as a cohesive group, do achieve an end result which society, as a whole, finds beneficial.

The only alternative to freely formed groups doing the physical things that need doing is to have those tasks done by the state, with the state attempting to carry out these productive processes as best it can. This fact is also basic to our thinking.

This voluntary cooperation among men for what may broadly be termed production—whether it involves operating facilities, selling, finance, or whatever it encompasses—requires many groupings of multiple sizes. The group may comprise an individual engaging the services of a few other individuals; it may be a small or large partnership or one of a myriad of other forms of association. But the most highly developed and usefully employed means of voluntary cooperation is the corporation, for in a corporation an individual may join the group as an owner or as an employee or as both. By its very nature and the rules which govern it, a corporation provides easy ways for persons to join and to leave, as owners or as employees. By utilizing the corporate form, the group can acquire a size needed to initiate and accomplish modern-sized jobs, a task to which no other form of voluntary association lends itself as readily. And by corporate organization the group can best ensure a continuity of existence.

Within any cooperating group of humans, each has a part according to his ownership, his interest, or his contribution, and it is necessary to have assignments and duties. Even at a church supper some people must provide the stove, the utensils, and the food; some must cook; some must serve; some collect and account for the proceeds; and some must give direction to the whole. Likewise in corporations, some people provide the facilities, some are given the task of getting the raw materials, some operate the machines, some account for the production, and some have the task of managing the various segments of its affairs—just as a university has its trustees, officers, faculty, and department heads. In a corporation these managing employees decide what should be made, who shall sell, and who shall account for its affairs; in a word, who shall prudently balance the interest of owners and employees in the group. Such decisions, however, are successful only if they also meet the requirements of persons outside the productive group who are being served by it.

Simple as this approach may be, it is clear, but all too easily forgotten, that only by cooperation and specialization can free men attain their objectives.

But with the formation of one group aimed at a certain task, other men are also free to form an organization to perform a similar task. The groups may multiply, several organizations may aim at the same purpose. In this way competition is born.

PRODUCTIVE GROUPS
AND "COMPETITION"

When one productive group earns profits to the benefit of its members, its profitability becomes, in substance, a broadcast invitation to other individuals to form a group to make the same thing or perform the same service. Thus competition begins to live.

In a reverse process, a group engaged in one activity may conclude that it is no longer in the interest of its members to continue that activity; therefore, this group stops one activity and begins to engage in another or sells out and joins up with another group or even disbands. This freedom of entry and, may I add, freedom of exit are all further evidences of the freedom of individuals to participate in the productive process.

These productive processes in America have developed amazingly under the freedom of groups to compete. The productive efficiency developed under the lash of that competition and its profit motivation has benefited our whole society. As these groups compete, a strong motivation to search for an improved way of mutual betterment is engendered and becomes a basic way of competing.

New products and new productive methods are

rewarding to the enterprising group which first develops them. The power of innovation begins to operate. Through such competitive innovation the needs of the consumer are best searched out and served. The end result is much greater production and far larger markets, served at competitive prices and at a competitive profit. True, the end result is also dislocations of people, of jobs, and even of entire industries. But this innovation also provides many more opportunities than it removes, as the growth in national job opportunities has shown. Thus this competitive activity is not only a constant spur to improving our living—it is progress itself.

We may observe, further, that the more groups we have and the greater the tasks performed by these groups, the more industrialized a nation becomes. A fairly useful way of estimating the industrial strength of a free nation is to observe the number and size of its freely formed productive groups. Moreover, the more of these groups there are, the broader are the areas of competition and the more complex are the criteria of competition. Competition, then, is not confined within a single industry or to groups making the same product. It extends to groups making products of different materials for similar uses, and it includes competition by all producers for the consumer's dollar. In a word, competition becomes interindustry. Likewise, competition is not confined within a nation's borders. It becomes international.

With respect to pricing and marketing, no longer is there the competition of a peddler with a pack of pots and pans on his back and a different price to every customer, nor the "perfect competition," sometimes suggested in textbooks. Today's competition is the competition of pricing policies, of quality, of consumer surveys, of mass advertising and of mass distribution devices, of research, and of production practices and conditions of employment. This kind of competition is the only kind that is workable in a society like ours, which requires large productive groups constantly moving forward to bring improved standards of living. The advantages to the consumer resulting from this naturally evolved competition are far greater than could ever be possible under the theory of "perfect competition."

Competition is the over-all performance of all of the people who work in the group. Let us not forget, therefore, as we proceed with our analysis, that we think in terms of identifiable, cohesive, and competitive productive groups of individuals—of people.

SIZE IN THE
PRODUCTIVE GROUPS

To understand these production groups of all sizes, it is vital to apprise ourselves of the fact that they are just that—of all sizes. This is so very important because these productive groups do not live alone or have isolated lives. Rules of group conduct, from whatever source promulgated, inhibit or enhance, each in its own way. What circumscribes one group affects the other. Sooner or late, directly or indirectly, they thrive or languish together. It is no small thing to select either the larger or the smaller ones for special benefit or restrictions and thus to meddle with the freedom of activity in these productive groups.

Let us look at these groups broadly—all 4.3 million of them in 1957 if you include individual employers with one or more employees.

In the aggregate, these 4.3 million voluntary productive groups consist of at least 44 million employees, or three-quarters of all our nonagricultural employment. They have at least 13 million individual owners who are their stockholders or proprietors. And, of course, many stockholders are also employees. It is obvious from this that the employees and

12

owners and their dependents make up the vast majority of all Americans—well over 100 million people. These millions of people are the persons whose interests are at stake in what we call "business."

Thinking of one corporation, such as United States Steel, or one industry, such as the steel industry, will not suffice for a true comprehension of the corporate foundations of a free society. In the aggregate, individual corporate units number 886,-000, of which 310,000 are in manufacturing. These corporations compose a family of many branches, with separate units of every size from small to large —the same unit being large to one mind and small to another.

It may be a convenience for the government to classify a nonferrous foundry with 100 or fewer employees as a small business, while it classifies a primary copper establishment as small when the number of employees is 400. In blast furnace units, the magic number is 500; in wire drawing, it is 750; primary aluminum, 1,000; and steel works and rolling mills, 2,500. It may be a convenience, but it does not detract one whit from the explicit fact that these groups are of all sizes from top to bottom and perform functions comparable to their size.

This is not a nation solely of big productive

groups, although it has a great many large groups of varying size which are constantly changing. It is a nation of voluntary productive groups of multiple sizes, with a constant flow of these groups in and out of the productive process. In 1957, for example, 332,000 of these 4.3 million groups went "out" and 365,000 different groups came "in." Of these 365,-000 new businesses, more than 136,000 were groups who used the corporate form.

Incidentally, there are more than 250 steel-manufacturing groups competing with each other for the privilege of keeping the market stocked with steel. There are twenty steel companies making steel structural shapes, although only four make the larger sizes of these shapes. There are sixty-four groups making hot rolled bars, fifty-nine making wire products, and so on, with various degrees of specialization throughout the groups.

United States Steel is the largest group of individuals productively engaged in our industry. In 1901, the year it was organized, it produced 67 per cent of the nation's steel. In 1958 it produced only 28 per cent. In 1907 United States Steel had 52 per cent of the nation's steelmaking capacity. Today it has 28.4 per cent. In this fifty-one-year period the capacity of United States Steel has increased more than 2½ times; nevertheless, that of its competitors has multiplied nearly seven times.

The American public has gradually become accustomed to larger and larger groups and has become convinced that big production groups are outstanding in reliability and in the quality of their products and services and are necessary to perform America's larger production tasks in research, in production, and in the procurement of raw materials.

This acceptance of large-scale production is a recognition of economic necessity. It shows that the American people understand the efficiencies of large-scale enterprise. They know, for example, that only a very large group could undertake to build an integrated steel plant like U. S. Steel's Fairless Works near Trenton, New Jersey—costing more than $400 million—and at the same time supply many more millions of dollars for a huge new iron-ore development in Venezuela. And they know that it is only by such economic expansion as this that we can make possible material progress for a growing America.

Yet the public, accepting size, is wary when it comes to what it thinks of as power, wherever and in whatever form that power exists. Many years ago, the American people, through their government, concluded that freely formed, competitive groups should not depart from a vital aspect of the competitive principle: that their production must be in competition with other groups. Public policy delineates and circumscribes what these voluntary groups may do competitively regarding their production, pricing, or distribution methods. To agree, for example, on the price of products or where they shall be marketed is not considered to be in the interest of a free society or permissible within our competitive principle. So we have such federal laws as the Sherman Act and the Clayton Act and many similar laws in the states. And even though individuals may differ greatly on what is adequate or persuasive evidence of competition between corporate groups, the general aim to maintain competition is agreed to be basic from a social point of view in a free society.

This desire to assure the maintenance of competition has tended to bring about oft-voiced concern that the "economic power" of large-scale production groups is harmful to smaller groups and that the competition of large enterprise would tend to squeeze them out of existence. That concern has been proved to be ill founded. We now have 886,-000 corporations where ten years ago we had 615,-000; twenty years ago, 470,000; forty years ago, only

320,000. It is also interesting to note that, during this period of growth in the number of corporations, the big corporations did not, as many people suppose, absorb a growing share of the total volume of business. In fact, the reverse was true. For example, a study by the Brookings Institution in 1953 revealed that in 1929, the before-tax profits of the 100 largest industrial corporations were 3.7 per cent of the total national income. In 1948, their profits made up only 3.3 per cent. Thus the profits of the large corporations represented a declining share of national income.*

There also exists an idea that the competitive positions of the biggest firms in any industry are always safeguarded by virtue of their very size. Again, the Brookings study proved that this was not so. It concluded that "the top was a very slippery place." The fact is that of the 100 largest industrial corporations in the country in 1909, only 29 were in this category in 1955.

Incidentally, in 1909, United States Steel's assets represented 22 per cent of all of the assets of the 100 largest industrial corporations in America. But by 1955, that 22 per cent had shrunk to 4 per cent,

---

* A. D. H. Kaplan, *Big Enterprise in the Competitive System*, Brookings Institution, Washington, D.C., 1953.

even though the corporation's assets themselves had more than doubled in this period. In other words, as new industries were born and as other companies grew, United States Steel, although itself a growth company, became less than one-fifth as large proportionately as it was fifty years ago.

But here I wish only to show generally what a vital part is played in the productive processes in our country by these voluntary groups we call corporations. I wish also to show how varied in size and complexion the group of business units as a whole really is, for in a free society the voluntary, competitive association of men doing specialized tasks is indispensable to the material growth of society. Their voluntary activities, as they have demonstrated, are the lifeblood of a free society and the building blocks upon which its material well-being rests. This is why our country produces about 50 per cent of the world's factory-made goods, although we are only about 6 per cent of the world's population and we are relative newcomers among the societies of the world. This is why we see communities and states all across our land vying with each other to get a productive, job-providing group—usually a corporation—to come in and set up shop in their town or their state.

There is no better evidence of the usefulness of these productive groups than the innovation and research they have provided—not only in terms of comfort, convenience, and the better life but also in terms of useful employment and of national safety. In 1953, production groups in America spent $3.7 billion on research and development. Last year that figure rose to $8.3 billion and it is expected to rise to $10 billion in 1961.

The vibrant capacity for innovation which voluntary men possess in their respective group activities can be seen when we reflect upon the multiplicity of products which are commonplace in our lives today and which were not in existence in 1900. It is further apparent when we note the steady increase in our total national work force and the shift—a matter of common knowledge—which has occurred from agriculture to industry, trade, government, and other nonagricultural pursuits. It is interesting to note further that more than 35 per cent of the sales value of United States Steel production in 1950, the last year we checked, was from the sale of products that did not even exist twenty years before.

Whether they think about it consciously or not, the men who forecast future miracles of production are relying upon the voluntary association of people in competitive groups, with their constant innovation, to bring about the progress predicted for the decades ahead. These forecasters assume that the voluntary, productive groups which are indispensable to our modern society will be allowed to continue—an assumption, but by no means an assurance, as we shall later see.

HOW A PRODUCTION GROUP OPERATES

Now then, how do these productive groups actually operate?

To answer that question in meaningful terms we must keep in mind that our businesses are groups of individual people—not monolithic masses of brute matter. These people formed or joined the group to improve their individual status by making and selling a product or supplying a service. To do this they must, in turn, establish relationships with other people in other groups, namely, the suppliers of products and services used in their work and the customers who buy the products and services produced by them. They measure their success in this undertaking by what we call a profit or a loss, depending, of course, on the outcome of their mutual efforts.

It is here that we find the standard by which the

success of the organization is primarily judged and the eventual success or failure of its work is determined. If the individuals in the group are cohesive and its members cooperate successfully among themselves, and if the group competes successfully with other groups, that success will be expressed by consumer purchases. The degree of that success will be evidenced by the growth of the group, its job-providing capabilities, and by the presence of what we call a profit.

Part of the profit will be paid to those whose savings and investment made possible the acquisition of the tools with which the group succeeded. The balance of it will be used to provide new tools to increase productivity further. Without profits there will, sooner or later, not only be no new tools but no tools at all. And this is the socially significant thing about profits most frequently overlooked—the increased wealth made possible by the new tools is shared by everyone. The physical things we all have —from electrical appliances and automobiles to living conveniences that, in fact, have become necessities—amply prove not only the necessity for those tools but also prove how widely the fruits of those tools are shared. It is a truism to say that all consumers benefit from improved tools of production, just as all consumers benefit by the efficient use of those tools in the fulfillment of consumer wants.

As we have seen, competition, whether it be for men, money, materials, or markets, is the continuing environmental factor which characterizes the relationship among these productive groups in our society.

It is also of interest to observe that only by benefiting other groups as well as society as a whole can any given group benefit its own members. This is true, because to live as a group, a service must be performed or a product made which another group or individual believes is desirable. Unless contracts when made are mutually beneficial to the buyer and the seller, the relationship will sooner or later benefit neither, and it will end.

In a very real sense, therefore, the members of a productive group profit only by benefiting others. And their position in the competitive scale is a measure of their success. Call this oversimplification if you will, but it is as basic as the group itself and as fundamental as material progress is fundamental.

But more about how the group operates.

In the beginning, a group of founding owners decide to get together for a common objective, usually using the corporation instrumentality. First of all, they provide the means with which to acquire the initial tools and facilities of production. Then they agree among themselves and with the initial board of directors who, in turn, must agree among themselves and with the management employees on plans and policies. The same process is repeated as the management employees reach understanding among themselves and with all of the other employees who are hired on who shall do what in order to accomplish the group's objective. As the group begins operations, it seeks and finds working relationships with other groups who are its suppliers and customers. At every point in time thereafter, these groups continue to develop and adjust their relationships in order for each to achieve its objective—and they can thrive only when they have the freedom to make such adjustments.

This process of reaching understanding within a single group is easy to describe, but understandably the accommodation of different points of view is not so simple, as all of us know. Understanding is accomplished by the group of individuals working together as a corporation, I believe, in much the same way as it is in any other free and voluntary association—whether that association be a local lodge, a committee to arrange a church supper, or even a group of small boys deciding how to play a game of sandlot baseball. As I think back upon it, it seems to me that either men or boys reach understanding in much the same fashion—by face-to-face discussion, presenting their points of view and reaching agreement on the basis of mutual understanding.

It is important to note that individual viewpoints and personalities are given full play in this process of reaching understanding. Each person in the group has an influence which is related to his role, his capacities, his experience, his judgment, and his persuasive abilities. He, in turn, is influenced by the attitudes and viewpoints of the others in the group. A particular individual may have considerable influence within a certain segment of the group, but his influence will be lessened with respect to those who are more removed from him in their activities. Naturally, the larger the productive group, not only the greater the communication problem but also the greater the available means of communication. Moreover, we must never lose sight of the fact that communication, like decision making, is a process constantly going on within the many smaller groups which compose a larger unit.

It matters not too much whether the over-all

group is large or small, because by mutual assent the span of an individual's relationships will cover mostly those matters—and the people concerned—about which he is considered to be competent. This, I think, sheds light on the problem of authority which troubles some people. *Who makes the decisions?* is a frequent question. In a voluntary association, be it a corporation or any other, those in the group must and do reach understandings, and thereafter authority is exercised according to such understandings. And through the same process these understandings are changed from time to time. This is the characteristic process of a democratic government, of a social lodge, of a civic organization, a professional organization, a university, and of a group in business.

This process of decision making and policy formulation and adjustment goes all the way from basic organization of functions to be performed to all of the other things that must be done in the business. Decisions on what is to be done—the group's definition of principles and objectives—are usually in very broad terms. From that point on, it is largely a question of how to accomplish the adopted objectives or how to achieve performance in accordance with the adopted principles. This is what we regard as administration of policy, and we believe it is wise and necessary to delegate widely the authority and responsibility to make administrative decisions. We believe it is desirable to solve problems as far down the line as possible.

It naturally follows that to the maximum degree feasible the views of the persons who will administer any kind of decision are taken into account before it is made. This process helps provide an adequate and clear communication of the decision itself.

In all of this, the basic purpose of the group—in the broad terms of competitive production—does not change, although it should be emphasized that the principles, attitudes, objectives, policies, and administrative guides must be subjected to constant review by the members of the group. These will change continually as new ideas and changed circumstances come along and as new people come into the group. In most instances the competition of other groups will all too clearly demonstrate when they must be re-examined and changed. And the group which has not exhibited the necessary flexibility will be penalized.

Thus competition is a cleansing agent; competition provides the most searching disciplines a free society can secure.

MANAGEMENT TECHNIQUES
IN UNITED STATES STEEL

The specialization which is essential within any corporation group requires what we call "organization." The organization of United States Steel is not unusual. We have a group of eighteen composing the Board of Directors. Twelve of these have the benefit of the differing experiences formed in association with other productive groups and have been associated with United States Steel only as directors. Three of the directors were formerly officer-employees and three of them are at present officer-employees. The board meets once a month. We also have an Executive Committee of the Board of Directors which is composed of twelve of its members which may exercise the powers of the board between meetings. There is also a Finance Committee composed of seven directors which is charged with responsibility for financial and accounting matters and meets twice a month. Next we have the Operations Policy Committee composed of the three officer-directors and seven other officers. These three top committees and the Board of Directors concern themselves with only the major expenditure and policy problems. They are the internal groups which have to make administrative decisions and to decide specific courses of action. All other committees process programs, exchange ideas, information, and viewpoints, and bring together a mutuality of understanding, particularly in the development and recommendation of policies or programs which cut across departmental lines or which affect the corporation as a whole.

The principal committee of this kind is the General Administration Committee which includes the members of the Operations Policy Committee plus operating heads of principal operating units or divisions. This committee meets monthly.

There are also specialized groups of employees each headed by an officer responsible for necessary services; seven of these officers are members of the Operations Policy Committee. These specialized groups include the following areas of responsibility: production, commercial, engineering and research, personnel services, international and raw materials, finance and accounting, legal, and public relations.

Many of the operations of the corporation are conducted by divisional organizations headed in each case by a president who, in turn, has his own organization. Each president reports to one of the officers who serve on the Operations Policy Committee.

What a corporation looks like on paper is one thing. But of greater importance is how does it come to life? What are the techniques which cause it to be successful? There are certain management techniques which a group originates or adapts to its use, just as there are special tools in any trade. In United States Steel, management techniques are the tools of our management trade. The committee system I have described is one of them and constitutes a part of our decision-making process.

Before discussing these tools, let me make two points clear. First, I have no notion that the techniques we use are superior to different techniques in other organizations. Each group needs its own techniques; therefore, it adapts techniques to its own use and thus improves its status as a group.

The main point I want to make here is that a group of individuals working together can and does develop the means of enhancing its common productive efforts.

I wish I knew a single word which would describe this whole process of creative production. By this,

I mean the myriad means which men employ to maximize their output and to economize the use of their time, materials and tools. Sometimes when we set about to list and describe these management techniques, we forget several important points. No one, however, should overlook the fact that the individuals using the techniques are equally as important as the techniques themselves. Thus we who are in the group always try to select the best qualified people; and once they have joined us, we do our best to see that they are well motivated to maximize their talents. I shall have considerably more to say about the opportunities for individual growth and development.

Then there is another aspect frequently overlooked. Able people, working with good management techniques and good facilities, need challenging objectives to tackle and need desirable policies with which to tackle them.

As I said before, we believe in the solution of management problems as far down in the organization as it is possible to find the knowledge and facts needed to reach a sound solution. This means two things. First, problems are solved as close to the actual site of the problem as possible. As a corollary advantage, the local organizations learn by doing and so improve their competence. This is one important means for developing decision makers in the group, enabling them to learn from a variety of experiences. Second, the higher levels of management are freed of problems that others can handle, so that they may devote time to the broader policy questions and to planning. Our way of working together has evolved over a number of years with a view to a greater degree of centralized policy making and of general coordination with the preservation of decentralized administration and operation.

To describe these management techniques fully would take a great many more pages than are here available. I shall, therefore, now merely mention briefly some of the most important ones upon which we rely.

First is our standard cost system, which serves as a kind of base for our other management techniques.

By enabling us to measure actual performance against reasonably attainable targets in any operation, the standard cost system provides the basis for effective cost determination, information relating to one of many pricing factors, information for raw material and facility planning, and for financial control and service to management.

31

Second is our planning program which estimates the potential markets for different steel products at various levels of demand and defines U. S. Steel's hoped-for place in those markets and how and where to produce most efficiently for such markets. It is a valuable guide in over-all planning, and it points the way to important cost savings.

Third is long-range facility planning, through which we take the limited funds we have available for replacement, modernization, and expansion and use them to maximum advantage in improving our competitive position and our performance as measured by our profit.

Fourth is our marketing program, through which we seek out those steel-consuming industries which are growing, those end uses which the community, as indicated by our market analysis, appears to prefer, and those product demands which offer the greatest long-range benefit. Market analysis helps us to achieve a reconciliation between these long-range objectives and the current distribution of our products.

Also available in the marketing program are the time-tested tools of advertising, of market development, of product development and a number of special promotional efforts.

The keystone of the marketing program, of course, is still the activity of the sales force out on the firing line. In this area, we are continually seeking new and improved methods of sales administration and control. Accordingly, our line salesmen are carefully selected, adequately trained, and backed up by the best commercial, production, and general management teams that we have been able to assemble.

Fifth is research and technology, emphasizing both fundamental and applied research and serving us importantly in two ways: (1) by developing new ideas and new products, improving our present products, and finding applications for them, it helps us to discover opportunities for our future growth and (2) by creating new methods and practices, improved techniques, and the means for better materials utilization, it contributes constantly to cost reduction and to increased efficiency of operation.

Sixth is a cost reduction program which enables us to improve our methods of operations. This embraces a standards comparison system to check costs of various operations so that, by breaking down costs and analyzing an unsatisfactory operation, we can rebuild and install revised practices. As an indication of the usefulness of this program, I might point out that in one segment of our operations—in a recent four-year period—the number of methods-improvement ideas increased from 11,500 to 83,000 per year.

Seventh is our incentive program—a major technique of management. In keeping with our policy to apply sound incentives where and when practicable, our incentive programs now embrace an employee suggestion plan, a patent award system designed to stimulate all employees to develop new and improved processes, a wage incentive program for the great majority of production and maintenance workers, a works management incentive plan, a sales management incentive plan, a general management incentive plan, a stock option incentive plan, and a savings plan for eligible salaried employees which features purchasing United States Steel stock.

A few comments on some of these management techniques will illustrate the value of all of them. For example, one objective of the standard costs activity is to find the manufacturing methods which will result in the lowest costs—all with an eye on broadening the market for our products. This requires advance engineering study—analysis of needed manpower, raw materials, equipment, and the sequence and flow of the work. These factors are studied for each small unit of a plan and then built up into larger aggregates—finally comprehending the entire organization and the entire product line.

Each department head has standards for measuring the performance of his responsibility in considerable detail, and against this are accumulated the actual cost of his operation in similar detail. The standard cost and actual cost are then compared, with the emphasis placed on those areas that are out of line with standards, and the differences are analyzed to determine the causes. These facts then are given to the operating management employees from the foreman level on up. Some reports are made daily, some weekly, and some monthly. Useful summaries of these data are also given to division executives and in still more summarized form to the headquarters people.

Not only is this system used to control costs, but it also serves as a planning tool. For example, the standards for required manpower are used to set up the work schedules for the men in the mills. They are used for planning raw-material deliveries and for laying out an orderly program of repairs and maintenance. Another use, which is invaluable, is in the designing of an over-all plan of operations under alternate given sets of circumstances. This tool is also one of the bases for engineering new facilities and for measuring their likely effectiveness. Standard costs are thus a full-cycle tool—important before facilities are acquired, vital to their usefulness, and useful as a signal to tell us when they should be replaced with more effective ones.

Encouragement given to employees to become stockholders inspires low-cost results and broadens the employees' interests in the success of the group as a whole. Being twice related to results, both as employee and owner, encourages an interest in the end result of the work of the group which operates to the interest of all concerned with it. Therefore, in recent years we began an employee savings plan for eligible salaried employees. Incidentally, many employees expressed interest in increasing their stock ownership in United States Steel prior to the inception of the plan. Under this plan, employees, depending on their length of service, can save up to 8 per cent of their pay in a fund to which the company adds one-half of the amount saved. All of the company portion and, if the employee so elects, one-half of his savings are invested in United States Steel common stock purchased on the open market. The balance of his savings are invested in United States government obligations. About 40,-

000 employees are participating in this program, or more than 90 per cent of those eligible. Most of these employees were not stockholders prior to the start of the savings plan.

A further word about research. This is one of our bright hopes for the future. Not only in United States Steel but in other major steel companies, research has been receiving more and more emphasis. The research push in the steel industry is symbolized by the large new research centers of our organization and of a number of our competitors. We compete in research, too.

Research offers promise of lower costs by reducing raw material costs, revolutionizing steel-making techniques, and enabling us to have lower investment cost per unit of product capacity. Thus research and the investment to which it leads contribute in an important way to our capacity to innovate, which I emphasized earlier.

Many of our research scientists are working on basic research projects seeking fundamental new knowledge not immediately related to steel production. Still others are working on new products in a continuing effort to make steel—which is already abundant and cheap—still more versatile.

In United States Steel more than 2,000 people

are engaged in research, not only in our main research center in Pittsburgh but also, on a coordinated basis, in laboratories of the separate divisions. Thus, research is one of the major preoccupations of our group.

THE HEART OF THE MATTER

Now I have mentioned these management techniques to throw some light on how free men in free association find ways to multiply their economic strength. I believe that there is no substitute for this voluntary private group as an economic means for securing production in a free society, whatever some people, frightened by complexities and by new economic assaults from Eastern Europe, may say. Without economic freedom it is not likely, in my view, that other freedoms would long endure.

I hope that by now these great families of small-, medium-, and large-sized corporate groups have come alive for you, for they are people and they constitute the economic bloodstream which feeds our free society. These groups are the providers—the suppliers and the creators of our free markets where customers are constantly deciding which of the groups serve them the better. In making his selection competitively, the customer pays for a job well done; and by paying, he directs the flow of production, the use of resources, and he stimulates the ingenuity of competing organizations—he rewards the better providers.

The whole process is a free society's way of disciplining itself.

But the heart of the matter is still not as clearly delineated as one would desire.

To me the heart of the matter is not that we have certain management techniques which do produce excellent results but that within voluntary groups of free men lie the genius and the will to originate and perfect those management techniques.

To me it is not that these corporate groups are the primary generative source of the capital formation of our land but that freely formed groups have, through their own internally directed efforts, the unrivaled capability for capital formation.

To me the heart of the matter, therefore, is not that corporate groups are the indispensable providers of the physical elements of our national well-being; the heart of the matter is that, through these freely formed and constantly evolving organisms of production, generative forces of great originality rise far above the individual imagination of any of its members, enhancing the role of *every* man and giving breadth and scope even to him who may be called the uncommon man.

To me, therefore, our common quest in this inquiry will only be fulfilled when we see not the storehouse with its bins of grain and its abundance which is our America but when we see the corporate key which enables free individuals cooperatively to build that storehouse and to replenish those bins.

But perceiving this corporate key is only our beginning. We must answer those who still ask: Do corporate groups stultify an individual and his creativity? Are corporate aims and those of labor unions essentially antagonistic? Do corporations or unions have too much power? What are the appropriate relationships between production groups and government and the community at large, and how useful are these private groups in the economic competition with the countries behind the Iron Curtain? For these questions, too, are the vital concerns of management.

CREATIVE MAN—
HIS WORK AND
THE UNION

THE INDIVIDUAL AND
HIS GROUP

In Chapter 1 we saw how men in a free society voluntarily join together in productive groups, how these groups compete, and how, through competition, society is benefited. We also observed that only in this way can free men do things in the magnitude required for our way of life.

But the heart of the matter was not so much that these corporate groups are the indispensable providers for our national well-being but that within themselves they provide generative forces of great originality, creating an unrivaled capability and giving breadth and scope to the capacities of each participant.

Thus we began to see creative man at work. But it is often said that creative man unduly loses freedom by joining a corporate group, especially one of large size, and that somehow his personal dignity and opportunity for personal growth are impaired.

Today some 44 million American people work for businesses of all sizes. And if they are losing more freedom than they are gaining from such association, especially in the larger units, it is time something is done about it.

At the outset I want to say that, speaking for only one "organization man," I believe that working in a corporation can contribute greatly to the freedom and growth of the employee; that an individual is not a machine but a warm, changeable, unique person who—partly because of his membership in a corporation group—is free and is encouraged to grow as a personality and can do so in reasonable relation to his abilities and ambitions.

Let us try to sketch our individual as he comes to work in the group. He has a name, an age, a family relationship and a home, a financial position, some formal schooling, and physical strengths and limitations. He brings a host of business and other experiences which will affect his work. He has a civic status and political beliefs, a religious faith, and habits of thinking on many matters, with old beliefs competing with new ideas in his mind. His culture and the heritage of national and racial strains

44

are wrapped up in him. He has anxieties, imagination and curiosities, and manners of action and speech. He can be reasonable or emotional, usually both. He has more or less of a capacity for tolerance of, faith in, and respect for, others. If we are lucky, he has a sense of humor.

He has great needs, ranging from things money can buy which he and his family need to the need for self-expression and self-fulfillment, which surpass material evaluation. He needs to be accepted as he is, for what he is—a respected, God-created, unique person.

He needs to know himself as best he can and to have his associates recognize his strengths and compensate for his weaknesses.

He needs, above all, *to grow,* for surely change will come and will present him with opportunity and challenge; change means either growth or decay. He needs to learn his job and how his specialty fits in with other jobs and to teach others about it.

At times he will have great need for specific direction, even for firm but fair discipline, for his group must turn out production at a competitive cost; and if he interferes or fails, he must be guided and encouraged by discipline.

He has many objectives—financial, moral, intellectual—and chooses to belong to many organizations to achieve them. His objectives change, and at times he will emphasize long-range, and at other times, immediate objectives. But a fundamental objective, constantly present, is to obtain the compensation which will bring to him and his family the desirable material things of life. In spite of self-centered drives, he is, nevertheless, capable of unselfish heroism; and yet on other occasions, seemingly incapable of recognizing and protecting his own self-interest.

As the passing years bring new strengths and new weaknesses and as he plays his part and observes the parts played by others, he needs to understand and to be understood.

But what is of overriding importance here is that he has voluntarily joined a group—to contribute to, and be rewarded by, the production and distribution of goods and services for society in general. And while we frequently find ourselves looking *at* him, we really begin to see him as a living personality when we look *to* him, not as a building block but as a sensitive person who is responsible and responsive —a vital part of a dynamic productive unit in a free society. His greatest needs on his job, and consequently the greatest needs of American industry, are that he have the opportunity to work, that he work effectively, that he be paid fairly, and that his relationships with his co-workers, especially with those he may be supervising, and with his own boss be friendly, satisfying, and productive.

His real dignity as a worker emerges as he gives strength to the group and gains strength from the group.

He is first a free man, free to join the group and free to leave, free to produce, to distribute, and to enrich his own economic and social values—if he chooses to stay.

The very joining and leaving is a dynamic process. In the year 1957, for example, over 25,000 individuals joined United States Steel and over 17,000 voluntarily left their jobs, a turnover rate typical of manufacturing industry as a whole. Those who left undoubtedly searched for greater opportunity elsewhere. While United States Steel does all it can to make its jobs more attractive, so do most other American corporations. This is in striking contrast to the restrictions which control the joining or leaving of a given production machine in a society which is not free.

But there is a great deal more. All that is offered is not just a chance to join, to work, and to quit. Just as society benefits from group production, so the individual in the group has opportunities to gain for himself an impressive set of values. His gains range from increased protection of his physical body in an increasingly healthy work environment to gradual improvement of his economic and social position. He even gains intellectual and spiritual values of satisfaction and service which any man might rewardingly choose as his highest aspiration.

The deeper truth is even more important than this. Not only does the individual have opportunity and encouragement to grow, but *if he does not grow, his service to his fellows in his group constantly diminishes.* My personal observation is that growth of the individual within a group compares very favorably with what it would likely have been if he had tried to render his service outside the group.

But what of the criticism that membership in a productive group requires conformity or some acceptance of the mores of the group?

There is no question that this is true to a degree— but it is also true of other noncorporate groups and it is natural and necessary. These limitations are not, however, as binding as many predetermined factors of the environment into which each one of us is born. In fact, it is quite misleading to regard as "restrictive" some conformity to modes of voluntary group activity. When individuals elect to associate in an interwoven pattern of cooperation to achieve production, there are bound to be some orderly means of getting the group's objective accomplished.

But within this orderly structure of organization there is great opportunity for diversified individual employee initiative and creativity. These are not only consistent with, but are absolute requirements for, achievement of the group objectives.

Now it is perfectly true that if the objective of the group is to grow "red roses," an individual who joins the group and who likes "pink roses" may feel a sense of frustration because he cannot plant and sell "pink roses." If the newcomer to the group desires to remold its activity to his own wishes, he asserts a position which may naturally find resistance in his fellows. What reason exists, they say, for us to do as he wishes? We like "red roses." Why should we, the older members of the group, accept his point of view? The point is that adjustment or conformity is a two-way street—and it is certainly not a peculiarity of corporate groups.

But that is not by any means the end of the matter. If our frustrated friend stays with the group, he has the opportunity of persuading his associates to go into the "pink rose" business. In fact, in 1958, nonmanagement individuals participating in our employee suggestion plan had 11,550 ideas for change accepted—ideas suggesting that we grow "pink roses" or how better to grow the "red roses," and the group was so anxious to get these ideas that it paid the individuals $375,507 for the suggestions. While many awards are small, last year, for example, at the Gary Works of United States Steel, two wage earners divided $32,000 for their suggestion on separating molten iron from slag as it comes from the blast furnace. This is, of course, considerably higher than their combined annual earnings. It illustrates that no job is too small to permit a man to better his own situation by bettering production for the group. In fact, whole departments and, in a sense, all departments are devoted to just that: to bringing about effective change in what the group is doing or what it is making.

Another way of evaluating what an individual gives up when he joins a productive group is to compare it with what he gains. I am not now thinking primarily of his personal financial position or even of his wages, insurance, pension, vacations, holiday, and other money benefits which he gains directly, whether or not, incidentally, he is in a unionized group. I am not overlooking these either, but compensation is characteristic of other types of employment too.

I want to emphasize, rather, a few of the features which more distinctively demonstrate that along with his economic growth, his stature as an active, free, responsible, and responsive human being also may thrive.

Qualifying for participation in training programs is only one of the many ways in which this happens. Industrial training programs have grown so rapidly and in so many directions that an increasing portion of what we once considered formal schooling is now taking place within American industry. The range of courses in the corporation, for example, includes the crafts (like bricklaying), advanced cost accounting, human relations, public speaking, selling, engineering, and even sending individuals back to colleges for refreshers and advanced management training. All of this is, of course, in addition to the vital day-to-day coaching, teaching, and learning that goes on right on the job. Our coworker increases his individuality as well as his usefulness by his participation in these training programs.

This leads to "promotion from within," another way individuals demonstrate their growth as distinct

of the difficulties we face today result from an insufficiently broad understanding by all people in our productive groups. Nevertheless, the creative individual who voluntarily joins a productive group does enlarge his horizon. He does widen his contacts with his fellow human beings. He thus matures as a person.

As our creative man matures, such group goals as industrial safety and industrial health take on additional significance. Protection of his physical and mental faculties becomes a higher value in his life. Since 1935, the severity and frequency rate of accidents in American industry has been cut in half; in the steel industry the data show an even greater improvement. To have a part in this means something to our maturing individual.

He also sees that the release of the group potential depends upon the quality of his own work, his understanding of its purpose, the free contribution of his creative ideas, the quality of communications with his associates, the respect which he accords to others and receives from others, the spirit and humor in which he undertakes his work, and his willingness and ambition so to develop himself that he can accept and perform increasingly greater responsibilities with added competence.

In recent years, because production by machine to some extent has replaced the old personal pride in workmanship, some people believe that all pride of achievement and personal interest in work has been lost. While this might seem so to the casual observer, the fact is that pride of accomplishment still exists. Today, achievement takes place through teamwork, as, for example, when members of a blast furnace crew take pride in working together to outdo another crew in competition for a production record. Also, as machinery replaces human drudgery in manufacturing, the personal pride in workmanship finds release in man's mastery of technology and the learning and use of skills he did not know or did not need in earlier days.

In short, I believe he begins to see more clearly that his cooperation with others toward the unified purpose of safe, efficient, and profitable production is a social function of the highest order. This also is personality growth, not its retardation.

To sum up, our group member grows as a person through adjustment, through training, and through doing important things with the group and for the group and hence for himself. True, all is not a smooth path to satisfaction of all desires. But here we consider the effect of group activity on individuality, and the point is that economic usefulness, which for much of life's activities must be a group activity, need not and does not stultify personality. In fact, our corporate associate has, in the Aristotelian view, provided himself with great opportunities for real happiness because his activities are virtuous.

Thus our individual takes pride in his work and pride in his association with his group—a very natural and a very wholesome thing.

THE "SEARCH FOR A BETTER WAY"

Now I readily agree that the improvement of human relations is an unending effort. In United States Steel a part of our own program is termed the "Search for a Better Way." It is a continuous operation. As its cornerstone we adopted a Creed of Human Relations and we try to live by that creed.

When we reach agreements on important matters, we frequently reduce them to writing as a guide to our future activities, a statement of our position as a group for the purpose of considering our affairs as a group. We, of course, do not claim perfection in wording or infallibility in concept for it, but we believe it is a major help in guiding our day-to-day relations among our fellow employees. Our Creed of Human Relations reads as follows:

Creed of Human Relations

We believe in the dignity and importance of the individual employee and in his right to derive personal satisfaction from his employment.

We believe each employee working toward attainment of the general business objective is an important member of the Corporation's team.

We believe each employee is entitled to receive—recognition and respect as an individual, constructive leadership, adequate information about his job and the business, prompt and fair consideration of his occupational problems, encouragement to contribute his ideas for improvement, opportunity to develop and advance, equitable compensation, and safe working conditions.

We believe each employee has the responsibility to— make the most effective use of his skill, effort, equipment, and time in the performance of necessary work—provide loyal and faithful service to other employees and the Corporation—and cooperate fully toward attainment of the general business objective.

Now the "Search for a Better Way" does not begin and end with the adoption of a creed. We realize that creeds can be made meaningful only if the individuals live in a climate in which they can reach the standards set forth in the creed. We began the

"Search" by testing the creed against the aspirations and opinions of our management employees. Through submission of a questionnaire to 26,000 members of management we tried our best to get uninhibited opinions. Careful analysis and appraisal of such replies by a university taught us how many members of management feel and what they think should be done in order to find a better way for the conduct of human relationships in our group. This information has led to adjustments in our organization structure and to the adoption of programs engendering personal growth and development of individuals which are, we believe, helping all of us as employees to live more useful and fruitful lives.

The "Search" program has enabled us to see something we all know, but to see it in bold relief—the importance of each individual in United States Steel and the effectiveness of a common interest in a common purpose as a unifying constructive force for production.

THE INDIVIDUAL
AND THE UNION

But we are far from knowing the answers to human motivation and behavior. Much has been accomplished by plan or even by accident or by the very restlessness of the human spirit. Nevertheless, we do know that many members of many productive groups, including United States Steel, have sought improvement in their group situation by joining unions.

While improvement in earnings may be a motivating force, it may also be that the main motivation is what we refer to generally as "working conditions," such as status in the group or seniority or enhancement of personal dignity. But joining a labor union may also be a response to a deep-seated psychological impulse—a quest for all the intangible satisfactions which we visualized in our description of the individual earlier.

Of course, the motivation may be simply to obtain a higher rate of pay, regardless of how it comes or what segment of society makes the payment. A higher rate of pay is associated in the minds of many in the group with ability to increase what we call security, or to provide more of the things we call generally by such phrases as "better living."

Whatever the reason, there are numerous and large union organizations of employees, and this bears heavily upon the efforts of the productive group itself to accomplish the purpose for which it was organized.

Fundamentally, we may think of the union as another group of individuals who have associated themselves for a purpose; where that association is freely and voluntarily made, it is similar to other associations of free men—although the purpose for which the association is made may differ from the purpose of a productive group.

If individual members of a production group feel that they can conduct relations with the management members of their group more satisfactorily by representation through a labor union—or if the administration of the group's affairs by the owners or the management employees appears to be unfair to the point where employees want a union to represent them—this is consistent with our basic concept of free association.

It is also true that many productive groups and the men associated in those productive groups find they can compete, produce and grow without need for a union, a group within a group if you wish. The average management individual in any group today would prefer, I believe, to provide that calibre of leadership, policies, and climate which all members of the group would so well understand and approve of, that they would feel no need for separate representation among themselves.

Nevertheless, where employees choose to be represented by a union, they and their union representatives can, if they will, contribute constructively to the voluntary, competitive, productive process. Where a union identifies itself with the productive group to which its members belong, it can well serve to improve management's awareness of the dignity, recognition, incentives, opportunities, and equities to which such employees are entitled.

But the activities and objectives of the labor union group should be consistent with the objective for which free men chose to associate as a productive group in the first place.

Somehow in our national anxiety to enlarge the opportunity for union organization and in our anxiety to build up something which we thought could operate as a check or balance to the growth of what we called the "power" of the productive groups of which I have been speaking, we as a people have far overreached our objectives—overreached to a point where the competitive principle is becoming submerged.

Unions now represent some 17 million American workers. Single unions, such as the United Steelworkers, Autoworkers, and the Teamsters, represent workers numbering a million or more. Union leaders compete with one another in making the largest promises, and to perform on such promises they apply powerful sanctions. The great power they possess has moved far beyond representing the members of competitive groups in their individual competitive situations. They now devote major portions of their energies to how over-all society should manage its affairs, how political parties—which are supposed to represent all the people, not just union members—should conform to their objectives. Their strength and influence in America today can hardly be overestimated.

Union leadership, by enforcing wage policies which apply to the millions of workers they represent, establish national wage patterns which in recent years have increased labor costs to a point where such actions now seem to be recognized, at least by many thoughtful people, as major contributors to inflation.

The power of labor unions and their dominance over a most essential part of the productive process of the many companies in entire industries, together with the effective collaboration among the unions, adds up to a force which no one company or even any one industry could begin to equal—a force which well surpasses the strength of any group of private organizations this country has ever known. And, as we observed before, people become wary of too much power.

THE MULTIPLE-COMPANY UNION AND THE COMPETITIVE PRINCIPLE

Earlier we have seen how productive groups are formed, how each strives to accomplish its work a little better and more efficiently and hence at a lower cost. We have seen how this ability and freedom to compete has been the great generative force behind our industrial strength. For in one way or another competition is the discipline that shapes our production—this discipline of cost competition in cohesive, competitive, productive groups.

But what is the effect of great multiple-company unions on the competitive processes?

Just this—and I can illustrate by using the steel industry as an example. The majority of hourly paid employees of practically all of the steel companies belongs to one union—the United Steelworkers of America. Hundreds of companies connected with production, distribution, or manufacturing of steel products and unrelated products have over 2,000 contracts with the same Union.

The results of collective bargaining between the companies and the Steelworkers Union have been characterized by unsustainable cost increases, major strikes, and government intervention.

Major steel industry-wide strikes of four to eight weeks occurred in 1946, 1949, 1952, and 1956, and a brief but costly strike occurred in 1955. An illegal seizure of the steel industry by the government occurred in 1952, motivated, I believe, by the objectives of union power.

In addition to the strike losses themselves, I see in such a pattern of experiences, and you may see too, that similar results in future years would be a great hazard to everyone—a hazard to each individual, the corporate production group, and the whole of free society itself. Here indeed we must "search for a better way" now.

It is this experience—and all that it implies for the future of economic freedom and opportunity and for the flexibility of groups voluntarily to compete with one another in the production of goods and services—that concern me. Continuing to drift as we are now, we may one day suddenly find ourselves in a vulnerable position so far as voluntary association, production, competition, and decision making are concerned.

A major function of the competitive principle is being impaired. It comes about this way.

The glacier-like forces of a powerful labor movement, including unions representing workers of hundreds of competitive groups, *adopt objectives that cut broadly into, and in fact largely contradict, the competitive principle itself.*

The original purpose of any competitive group becomes secondary, if not completely lost, as the labor union activities are extended far beyond the scope and purpose of the productive group—extended across multiple groups of intercompany and interindustry areas and even into government. *The unhappy by-product of this movement is that its results are made to appear—to some people—as a defect in the competitive group method of production itself.*

There need be no antagonism between the interests of the whole group, namely, the stockholders and all employees on one hand, and a part of the group, the union members, on the other; and, I think, inherently there is none. Many times it would appear so, but I am sure differences between the members of the same group can be resolved so long as the interests of the over-all group remain identified and paramount. Rather than inherent or class

65

antagonism there is a basic identity and affinity of interest in competitive production—all members of the group are in the same venture, each has need basically for a real concern for the welfare of the others.

It is true that union employees in a productive group may desire more of the proceeds which come from the customers who buy the product of the group—more than the owners or management employees are convinced it is possible for them to receive without impairing the ability of the group to compete. Such an issue should be susceptible to reasonable analysis and settlement, consistent with the objectives of competitive production for which the total group organized in the first place. In such a framework no prudent and well-informed employee would contemplate insisting upon that share of the proceeds which would make the enterprise noncompetitive or a share that could be distributed only at the risk of destroying the capital upon which the very life and service of the corporation group and the jobs of its members depend.

When employees do strike, do they strike because of disagreement with owners or management employees of individual production units on how the affairs of the group will be carried on, or do they sometimes strike for reasons related to union rivalry or national prestige or someone's economic concepts?

We in the steel industry know only too well that the very scope of labor negotiations—where one union represents thousands of separate employee groups and insists upon broad application of substantially uniform conditions of employment—becomes so complex and so remote from so many of the individual units involved that the union employees in any one group never do have a realistic opportunity to discuss their own conditions of employment with the owners or the management employees.

And once a strike is called—especially in a critical industry like steel—there arises a clamor that the nation cannot afford the luxury of a strike. It must be settled at all costs. The public, the press, the political climate, and the government—all place pressure on the industry to come to terms. Then when the companies, after taking a strike of many weeks' duration, comply with the clamor for steel products and after increased labor costs are reflected in steel prices—as they frequently are—*then* comes the criticism that the steel companies "gave in" too easily and passed on the higher costs to the public in the form of higher prices.

67

When, moreover, a strike is ended, many of the corporations, usually the smaller ones, are compelled by union demand, and by the practical necessity to begin operating again as soon as possible, to accept a settlement and sign a contract in the composition of which they had no genuine voice, a contract whose terms they understand only in a general way. This fact of business life in the middle of the twentieth century is so freely recognized that it even appears in the public press. Some years ago, following an agreement between the Steelworkers and Bethlehem Steel Corporation, an able and competent district director of the union was sent, according to a published report, to negotiate an identical settlement with the Colorado Fuel and Iron Company, another steel company. "I'm going to New York," explained this director, with a grin, "and I'll see the Colorado Fuel and Iron people. I'll say to them, 'We want the Bethlehem Formula.' They'll say to me, 'What is the Bethlehem Formula?' Then I'll pound the table and I'll say, 'What the hell are you trying to do—break the union?'"

In the ensuing years since this episode, settlements have been enforced in much the same atmosphere.

Is it therefore time to raise the question of

whether the original purpose so many sincere people had in fostering the cause of unions has somehow gotten out of hand? Should we ask whether nationwide wage policies, industry-wide strike power, the ability to shut down whole industries and to bring economic America to its knees is necessary or right?

Are the losses thus incurred a good or sustainable result when they come from a multiple-company labor policy of "charging all the traffic will bear" regardless of the effect on the individual production centers or their ability to compete and produce and, most unhappily, regardless of the effect upon the principle of group competition itself?

How have the individual production groups reacted to the power of multiple-company unions? They have felt compelled in many instances, at least the larger of them, to join in one way or another to achieve even a semblance of balance in bargaining strength. The smaller units have done their best to try to learn what is going to happen to them as a result of a bargaining process in which they have little or no voice. The objectives of the individual productive groups are practically lost sight of in the shuffle.

Put yourself in the position of the owner, manager, or the employee of one of the many thousands of firms in the transportation business which is now subject to the jurisdiction of the Teamsters Union. Or, put yourself in the position of a business unit which may be subject to the strength and will of that union if its idea of one union for all transportation employees—with the policemen and hospital workers of New York City thrown in for good measure—were to be realized. What chance would you have?

The matter goes beyond this. The ultimate results of these union policies—greatly influenced by interunion rivalry—have gone so far that they approach the molding of society to the unions' own ends.

Justify this if you will by saying that it is but evidence of a social force in which the lower-income groups at last receive recognition and that they do but mold society to greater ends. But contrast this with how society actually achieves its improved standards of living—through the encouragement and growth of the individual voluntary groups and their production, not their obliteration.

Nevertheless, present-day multiple-company bargaining has won such widespread adoption that we ought to examine further and ask whether its presence does not indicate a merit which outweighs the demerits which some see in the growth and power of unions. Is it not, we may well ask, a realistic answer in the world of today?

It may be asserted in favor of this practice that the negotiation of uniform conditions of employment merely sets standards under which it is assumed all the productive units involved may compete. However, the assumption that employment costs do not affect the competition of productive groups simply is not true. Companies are continually moving from one place to another in this country and even abroad for a variety of reasons, it is true, but among those reasons a most prominent one is the need to be competitive. As one of the largest determinants of over-all costs, employment costs vitally affect the capacity and flexibility of companies to compete and grow. A good illustration of this is the foreign competition presently capturing some of our markets because of our noncompetitive labor costs.

What is overlooked is the basis of competition itself, the need for a production unit to compete as a cohesive whole. Acceptance of the great union force cutting across the competitive units overrides the larger benefits which come from the productive process when all the members of a productive group are working with a unity of purpose.

We hear of the results of such unifying devices as the Scanlon Plan and the Rucker Plan and of a variety of other incentive plans, all of which are successful to the extent they succeed in identifying each employee with the other members of his group and with the purpose of the group as a whole.

Interestingly enough, in many cases, employees of a group understand this situation. They agree to do whatever is necessary to remain competitive when they grasp the relation between competition and their work. They adopt all sorts of cost-reducing devices to help save their work opportunities and the enterprise and enable it to compete. One case, in Amesbury, Massachusetts, which received public notice recently involved the union and some of its individual members buying control of a small hat company, which was about to be liquidated. By this action they saved the jobs of 325 workers.

The union leader himself, freshly impressed with his management responsibilities, said, "First, we must make a profit . . . then, we should pay $2 a share, or if the profits justify it, $3 a share." He also recognized that additional income should go first into building reserves and then into gains for the workers. He also recognized the need for research and market development. The union official was beginning to understand his new responsibilities.

I do not suggest that increases in labor cost, of and by themselves, cause all dislocations, and I recognize that some economic displacements may also be evidence of progress. But we must ask ourselves whether many business casualties are not victims of the denial of free opportunity to produce competitively.

The temptation to regard union-induced limitations on competitive production as social progress is less attractive when we realize that, over the last fifteen years or so, we have been undergoing a cost-push type of inflation—in large measure as a consequence of out-of-line labor cost increases forced by major labor unions. In the period of 1940 through 1958, primarily as a result of labor negotiations, hourly employment costs for our own company have increased at a compound rate of 7.9 per cent annually. During the same period the increase in output per manhour—a measurement which always overstates productivity—averaged about 2 per cent annually—the difference being necessarily covered by such price changes as competition permitted.

In addition to all of the adverse impact this has had domestically, it is beginning to show in major areas an adverse impact upon the ability of American industry to compete with foreign production. An eye-opening example of this was given to me recently by the Worthington Corporation of New Jersey. Their figures show that it costs them nearly 2½ times as much to make a small-sized centrifugal pump in their American plants as it does in their lowest-cost plant in Europe. From 1953 to 1958, their costs for making two sizes of pumps and a medium-sized air compressor *increased,* in the United States, by 35 to 49 per cent; while the cost of manufacturing these same items in Europe *decreased* by 2 to 5 per cent. Thus in Europe, costs on these products are declining and the competitive position of European producers is improving, while in the United States these costs are rising tremendously and the competitive position is deteriorating rapidly.

In our own steel industry we know that the trend in certain steel imports seems to be sharply up and the export market for higher-cost domestically produced steels is certainly not flourishing. Why? Certainly part of the reason is explained by the fact that European steelworkers are paid about one-third and Japanese steelworkers about one-seventh as much as American steelworkers.

German wiremakers have produced barbed wire

in their plants, shipped it across the Atlantic, and sold it in Cleveland at approximately $40 a ton less than barbed wire made right in the area. The Japanese purchase American scrap, haul it back to their mills in the Orient, manufacture it into finished products, reship it back across the Pacific, and still undersell American producers by as much as $29 a ton, for example, on reinforcing bars for the building industry.

It is said that there is also wage inflation in other countries, but in the period from 1950 through 1957, the American steelworker received more in wage increases than the German steelworker received in total wages at the end of that period. During the steel industry's three-year agreement with the United Steelworkers ending in June 1959, employment cost for the steel industry increased 81 cents an hour and, at the end of the period, was more than $3.60 an hour. During the same period employment cost in German steelmaking plants increased 19 cents to a total of about $1.10 an hour.

When we realize that employment cost is the largest of all costs in production of goods and services, representing 75 to 80 per cent nationally, it is easy to see the adverse effect which large labor cost increases, arising from demands of powerful labor unions, have upon the ability of the members of American production groups to produce, compete, grow, and provide employment.

Recognizing such expedients as tariffs, quotas, subsidies, controls, freezes, and all of the other temporary "ways out," sooner or later we shall have to face up squarely to one undeniable fact: that American workmen today in many areas are pricing themselves out of markets, or to put it even more accurately, that America, as a nation, is *costing* itself out of many markets. This, too, is part of the price we pay for the multiple-company unions.

Recent Congressional hearings have raised a variety of other questions regarding activities of some labor unions upon our free society and upon individual freedom. But here I am trying to examine only their effect on the unity, cohesiveness, and purpose of the competitive group.

To their credit, some unions have, on occasion, tempered their demands to the economic conditions faced by a competing group. But the competitive way requires more than acts of sufferance by union leadership, whose industry-wide decisions may or may not be in the interests of the members of the individual productive units within the industry. *It requires, rather, that the individuals in a group, whether or not they are union members, be so wholeheartedly a part of the group itself that they will be able freely to join in, and advance the competitive interests of the group.*

Many, including management or, should I say, especially management, must share responsibility for the breakdown of the cohesiveness of the competitive, productive units in our society. The real challenge to all the individuals in each group—and again a challenge to management especially—is to find means through which all members of the group can be motivated toward more effective fulfillment of the group's objectives. This is the best way to improve the real earnings of all the employees and the way to real national growth.

THE ROLE OF THE UNION IN THE FUTURE

We know from our analysis and from our experience how national security and growth in national wealth are achieved. Today, more than ever before, we know that from an international viewpoint there is no time to be lost in energizing our productive capabilities—even if we visualize only a friendly competition from abroad. When we see the militant, purposeful competition which seeks to overwhelm the voluntary way, the matter becomes vitally pressing.

Understanding the structure and motivation of this voluntary way of production—and realizing how the greater labor unions are now hampering our productive process—is a matter whose importance can hardly be overestimated. If for no other reason than that employment costs represent 75 to 80 per cent of all costs and that costs are, broadly speaking, one way of measuring the effectiveness of human endeavor, the matter is worthy of our best attention.

After all, this is a competitive world, and it is in the interests of every member of our free society, including union members, to keep it that way. There need be no fear that our American workman will not acquit himself satisfactorily in competition as a workman—if he is permitted to do so.

Somehow within the union groups themselves there must be achieved a greater understanding of how production requires a unity and integration within each self-generating group. Many of our thoughtful union friends are undoubtedly concerned with the broadside effects of their policies and organizations on these productive units. Their responsibility is the greater because of the power they wield.

As the remedy for this situation, some may suggest that policy considerations within the great unions themselves can provide satisfactory resolution. This certainly would help. Others may suggest some form of decentralization within the multiple-company unions. This would, no doubt, be completely unacceptable to some union leadership. The only suggestion I now make is that the creative voluntary way of production is such a national asset that its preservation and improvement should receive the consideration of thoughtful men everywhere—including union leadership—and that in some way private policy and even public policy must recognize that labor practices which impair the competitive principle are incompatible with a free society.

Even now we see advanced in Congress numerous proposals for controls of one sort or another which would lead to Washington control of wages and prices. Even now we hear of such things as so-called "administered prices" and we hear the claim that the existence of the larger business units causes all sorts of economic evils such as inflation, upon which the business units actually have a reverse effect when they are free to act naturally.

If there ever was a case of mistaken identity, of attributing effects to wrong causes—this is it.

CITIZEN MAN—
HIS GROUP AND
HIS GOVERNMENT

INDIVIDUALS, GROUPS, AND GOVERNMENT

The last chapter of this book is like the third leg of a three-legged stool. It sustains the whole.

The first two chapters sought to show how members of a free society can provide modern industrial and physical requirements only by means of voluntarily formed productive groups of individuals. If a group is successful, a continuing constantly changing productive unit results. Other groups are similarly generated by the example of the first and thus competition is born. The multiplication of these groups creates a highly competitive economy. In Chapter 1 we saw how competition operates among integrated groups which, for convenience, are usually organized as corporations.

While some other form of productive effort may serve the objectives of a compulsory society, in a free industrial society—or one at least reasonably free—we have found no substitute for voluntarily formed productive groups, primarily corporations.

We also considered how individuals work together in these groups, how members of a group grow as individuals and how the individual and the group gain strength from each other.

We saw how an ever-present competition between integrated, cohesive groups, which we have described as the competitive principle, is not only the preferred rule of our society but is the swiftest and most effective means of attaining society's physical needs. In all of this we saw people, banded together and motivated by their own self-interest, exercising great ingenuity for production and becoming the innovators and the generators upon whom society's physical betterments and, in fact, its very safety depend.

We also saw how achievement of the group's objective depended upon the creative productivity of the individuals within the group and upon the cohesiveness of the group effort. And we saw how division within the group is inevitably a restriction on production.

Finally, at the conclusion of the last chapter, we saw how the activities of powerful multiple-company unions, with interindustry affiliations, cut across and thwart the operation of the competitive principle, even to the point of endangering that principle.

Against that background, this third chapter seeks to examine the relationships between the voluntary corporate groups and government and between these groups and the community as a whole.

We have been looking at the individual in the group as a voluntary man and as a creative man. Let us now look at him as a citizen man—as a member of society with plural interests and activities. He is a member of many groups, but he is first of all a citizen of his country. This naturally involves many vital facets of his life, but here we consider our citizen man only as a member of a productive group. As such, he is keenly interested in the relations between his group and his fellows in government, that is, the other members of society who are elected or appointed to enact the laws or to administer the laws or to interpret the laws. For our citizen man knows by long experience that his group will be greatly affected by the rules relating to the group activities. Thus his own welfare, both as a member of that group and as a citizen in society, will be vitally affected. In fact, he knows that what his group can contribute in society is to a great degree circumscribed by these rules.

Let us first examine, therefore, certain things which our citizen man observes when he turns his eyes toward government and looks at government's effect upon one of his vital interests—his work.

The relations between government and the thousands of productive groups are innumerable. Each group, depending on its size and place in the economic life of our nation, has contacts with a great many departments and agencies of government; it files hundreds of reports and in many instances benefits from the response it receives in government statistics; it complies with the orders, pronouncements, regulations, and opinions of the Securities and Exchange Commission, the Federal Trade Commission, the Department of Justice, the Labor Relations Board, the Interstate Commerce Commission, and many other Federal and State regulatory departments and commissions. Altogether it leads, regulatorily speaking, a rather distracted life. But again, our central thought will not be advanced by the impossible task of pausing to look at all existing regulations and promulgations. Being a member of a productive group, our citizen man wants to get on with his work.

In getting on with his work, he is firmly grounded in the knowledge that his group, without regard to its size, needs tools to aid production. He and his associates understand tools. They see at a glance how a new tool, for example, a steel plant or a jet air liner or an earth-moving machine, can increase production. They also can see how freedom to obtain and replace tools enhances their group efforts. They know that their group and members of other similar groups have only what they produce. The better performance of useful work profitably to improve their individual status is the basic reason they formed the group or joined it in the first place.

To get these tools, they need to induce others to rely upon their group and help supply the necessary funds, and they know these others will rely upon them only when there is promise of reasonable security for their investment. And they know that these others, whom we call stockholders and bondholders, will furnish the tools only if they have a hope of getting dividends or of getting back what they loaned with interest.

The members of any group are aware that other groups are also looking for tools with which to produce—and that there is competition between productive groups, not only with respect to the products made but for the tools and the wherewithal to acquire tools.

Against this need, what may the members of a productive group reasonably expect of their fellows in government, whom they know wish to be responsive to the interest of the whole of society? Substantially, these things: first, an understanding of their usefulness as a productive group. This carries with it a realization on the part of their fellows in government that a free society, if it is to remain free, cannot exist without these competitive corporate groups. They may also ask for an understanding of what motivates these groups and enables them to function. They may also ask that, when their fellows in government establish the general rules of conduct which these myriads of groups must follow, they somehow develop an appreciation of what it is that they do.

ECONOMIC GROWTH AND GROUP COMPETITION

I doubt that there is anyone who is not affected by or interested in our national growth. I suppose also there is common agreement that national growth may be achieved only through the work of people—productive people, joined together and gainfully motivated. Since these groups constitute our major instrumentality for national growth, how can we increase that growth without increasing the number, size and effectiveness of our productive groups?

If we have an understanding of group production on the part of our fellows in government and if they are interested in national growth, as I am sure they are, which of two alternatives would they take, for example, in the matter of taxation?

Would the approach be to shape tax policies so as to induce the corporate group to acquire more tools of production, to get the best tools possible and keep them up-to-date and thus create more of the physical things which society needs? Or would the approach be to look upon the group primarily as a source of maximum possible revenue and thus deprive the group of the means of acquiring the tools of production?

Now this is not to say that corporate groups should not be taxed. And it is not to say that everything is wrong with our present approach to taxation. But it is very doubtful whether the taxing of corporate groups has been approached from the standpoint of increasing their productiveness. If it has, the execution of the policy leaves something to be desired.

Consider the matter of depreciation on physical

tools in a period of inflation. Is it conducive to greater productivity to assume that a machine which is used up in production can be replaced by a third or a quarter of a machine—and the same production maintained? Yet that is precisely the result of the present tax laws on depreciation.

An example will help. Back in 1930, United States Steel built an open-hearth plant which cost about $10 million. Today it would cost more than $64 million to replace that plant. Through depreciation we recovered the original $10 million that we spent on this facility. Taking into full account the somewhat greater production of the new plant, it still cost more than 4½ times as much, per ton of capacity, as the original facility did.

The tax law in this case would seem to assume that our group can consume in production a furnace and then replace it with less than one-fourth of a furnace and still do the same production job.

How much better from the standpoint of increasing the productiveness of the myriad of groups all over the country would it be to approach tax policy concerning depreciation from the standpoint of generating greater national growth rather than in a way which subtracts from the group the productiveness which it already has. Every other free industrial nation has adopted depreciation tax laws more realistic than those of the United States. The rapid growth of West Germany, for example, illustrates the results of such laws.

We cannot take the time in this brief discussion to develop what is one of the most seriously needed and least understood requirements for inducing greater productiveness throughout our land. For want of a better description I will term this "the unexplored art of taxing for national growth."

Both our national safety and our national productiveness depend upon new and better methods of production and new and better products. These in turn depend increasingly upon the activities in the research segments of our nation's productive corporate groups. Last year it is estimated $8.3 billion was spent for this purpose. Can you think of a better way of inducing these voluntary groups to expend more for research and development than by making it possible for them to do so through some form of increased tax encouragement?

I realize that many will differ with respect to what is or is not a fair method of taxing corporations. But if new tools and innovations are the principal source of our increasing productiveness, then I ask in what better way can the productive strength of each individual group be increased and therefore the composite productive strength of the nation be increased than by restraining unnecessary government expenditures and by reorienting our thinking toward taxation to aid growth? Would this not also serve to increase our productive base for needed revenues, far more than does the "ability to pay" idea?

Still examining what we may reasonably expect from our fellows in government, let us look at the question of competition between groups, remembering that the great majority of Americans is associated with one or more of the many families of enterprise called "American Business."

First of all, each group was originally formed to compete successfully—to do something a little more usefully or a little better or a little cheaper, which would induce purchasers of a product or a service to buy from its particular group. Since the activities of the group are centered around production and distribution, its members are constantly aware of what is needed to induce a buyer to buy. They know, for example, that price is a vital element in competition and that if they can reduce their costs so as to be able to sell profitably at a lower price, they can increase the buyer's inducement to buy from them.

They also know the value of quality and the value

of new equipment capable of producing that quality, or service. They know the importance of having a product available *when* it is needed and of locating equipment to make their products available *where* they are needed. And they know the value of the many other elements which enable them as a group to compete for a customer's favor.

The essence of their ability to compete relates fundamentally to their ability to make determinations relating to these elements of competition, price included. Thus, when some of their fellows in government—who apparently fail to understand how competition works for the American people—suggest that the members of the productive groups give up the right to determine the price at which they will sell products and the right to modify those prices quickly in response to the swiftly moving and innumerable changes in all kinds of competitive conditions, two results are immediately apparent to the members of productive groups. First, the major purpose for which they formed the group in the first place or joined it—the incentive of competitive, productive self-interest—is largely removed. They know how vital the existence of these competitive groups is in our free society, how their freedom to act and the discipline of competition are synonymous with

93

our progress as a people. All of this is endangered. Second, they know that someone must establish prices and that if competitive groups are not permitted to do this, it will be done by their fellows in government.

And as Hamlet said, "Ay, there's the rub." They know that, once started, government elimination of competitive factors never stops and that, however small its infringement to begin with, it inevitably grows. They know that this elimination of competitive factors cannot be imposed on any one competitive group without being imposed on others. They know that identifying products for price controls is far from simple, that there are alternatives and substitutes for products and that thus the establishment of the control of one price for one product in one industry quickly and inevitably leads to control of other products in other industries.

They know also that a progressively larger and larger government organization will be required to establish prices. They know that sooner or later, and probably sooner, all economic activity will be under the same controls, including wages which are the price of labor; for the nation's wages are 75 to 80 per cent of costs, and costs are a primary factor of prices.

And furthermore they know this: when price controls are imposed—if they ever are—and when price competition is thus eliminated—if it ever is—and when government takes over the decision making with respect to prices—if it ever does—they know that the heart of the competitive principle, and the productive system they once had, is a "gone goose."

But, true as all this may be, it does not point up the remedy to their fellows in government for some of the problems which these gentlemen have—and those are real problems. Inflation is not the least of these.

INFLATION

Any time and anywhere two or more individuals in our present-day American society are gathered together, whether they are concerned with national problems or not, the question of inflation is almost certain to arise. It comes up at the grocery store, the auto salesroom, in Albany, or Washington, or even, I am sure, in the councils of great universities. It pushes hard on everyone's thinking because it involves money and credit, wages, prices, taxes, costs, profits, competition, and all kinds of economic situations—foreign as well as domestic.

95

Upon every productive group inflation has exerted a pervasive, insidious influence for at least twenty-five years. And what do the members of productive groups expect of their fellows in government in respect to this matter? As I have indicated, they do not expect that inflation can or should be corrected by placing ceilings on prices. But the members of the group realize that there is a problem and that it is a problem their fellows in government must understand if they are to deal with it.

We have no inclination or time or adequacy to delve into all aspects of inflation which so beset the entire community. But those in government know that the activities of government itself can induce the cheapening of the dollar. Spending more than the government receives in revenues, and thereby constantly adding to the money supply, is an easy and quite certain way to monetary inflation. But here we make no effort to express our citizenship voice in suggesting what government should do. Our interest lies in having our fellows in government understand how what they do affects our nation's productive groups.

There is one point, however, upon which I believe we can be helpful. Lately more and more realization of the powerful upward pressure of great collective bargaining unions on price levels is coming to be realized. But it is not so clearly understood that this effect is brought about because of the debilitating and inhibiting effect which union power has on the competitive principle.

The corporate groups to which I have been referring, organized to produce and compelled to compete, have a self-regulating effect upon each other in the matter of prices. But when the nationwide multiple-company union presses forward with a wage demand which, like an advancing glacier overwhelms all before it, the competitive principle which normally regulates prices must likewise yield ground and begin to function again at a higher level.

In support of the policies of these great union forces, the point has been made that, in spite of their inflationary effect, the unions' upward pressures on costs improves the efficiency with which the community utilizes its manpower and other resources. I am personally not persuaded that this idea has validity. I mention only one point with respect to it. There are two 10-year post-war periods —1920 to 1929 and 1948 to 1957. One precedes the establishment of great union forces and the other follows. The terminal years of both periods were high-level prosperity years. The reported increase in the private economy's productivity over the first 10-year period was 23.1 per cent, and in the second period it was 23.0 per cent. If the power of unions to raise wages has the effect of speeding the growth in productive efficiency, one would expect at least some evidence to be visible in the comparison of these two periods. I might add that the standards of efficiency in many companies which have no great union pressures are certainly just as high as those which do have that pressure.

Moreover, if this reason for the wage activities of great unions is valid, there should have been generated increases in the profits of our productive groups in recent years which at least would have kept up with the parade of wage changes on something like a proportional basis.

The fact is, however, that only twice during the 1950's have the after-tax profits of all corporations been as high as they were in 1950. In all other years they were lower and government reports show that, in 1958, they were only about $18 billion, almost $5 billion less than in 1950.

The same government reports also show, however, that compensation of employees, throughout the nation, has risen by $100 billion since 1950 to an estimated $254 billion in 1958. So I leave it to the reader: Whence cometh this cost-push inflation?

From their fellows in government, therefore, the members of productive groups are entitled to expect understanding of this glacier-like force of union power, understanding of its effect upon the stability of price levels and upon the prices the consumer pays, understanding of its effect upon the payments government makes for products and services which it buys and upon the payments made to government employees and for pensions, and understanding of its effect upon the revenues required to conduct the affairs of government.

With that understanding, our fellows in government must know that they bear at least partial responsibility for inflation. When and how they will try to correct these conditions I do not hazard a guess, although I am not one who believes that they have lost either the will to tackle the job or the ingenuity to accomplish it.

What is *not* understandable to members of a productive group, however, is why some of those concerned with the matter should suggest the price controls we have just discussed, which would weaken the productive strength of the thousands and thousands of corporate groups all over the country, as a corrective measure for the government's spending more than its revenues and as a remedy for the effects of great union power. Weakening the competitive principle still further as a remedy for a condition which has already weakened it is sheer nonsense.

It has been suggested that the remedy for inflation is to establish wage and price policy at a national level. But how can this be done without the government's substituting its decisions for the disciplines of competition?

Is it too much for all of us as citizens and as members of productive groups to ask that our fellows in government understand that the further enhancement of the power of larger and larger unions, the further weakening of the competitive principle, and the further establishment of single national decisions affecting wages and prices all point in one direction? And that direction is toward the establishment of complete planning and production by government—toward artificial shortages, peacetime rationing, and regimentation of the entire economy. The drift is in that direction and it is not an inviting one.

And may I add that all the implications attributed to so-called "administered prices," if anything charitable can be said about them, are confusions of thought and an evidence of great misunderstanding. So-called "administered prices" have nothing to do with the fiscal and monetary policies of government which affect inflation or with glacier-like forces of great unions which have contributed to the inflationary spiral, as I believe the academic community is fully aware.

Having a policy with respect to pricing under which prices are posted for a period of time is essential to modern marketing, and such prices are just as surely market prices and evidence of competition as the comparatively few widely and rapidly fluctuating commodity prices which some call "market prices."

Moreover, as to the charge that so-called "administered prices" have risen more rapidly than so-called "market prices," the fact is that, if the whole inflationary period since before the war is taken for examination and not just some period beginning with relatively depressed "administered prices," the degree of increase in these prices is somewhat less than in the so-called "market price" groups, although the difference is not too significant.

BUSINESS GROUPS AND POSITIVE GOVERNMENT PROGRAMS

But more about the relationship of productive groups to government in this rapidly changing world. With great nations now utilizing their not inconsiderable resources to advance political ends, is the profit-motivated voluntary productive group a basic foundation upon which our fellows in government can safely rely? Or must the voluntary way be abandoned and some new instrumentality be developed which will mean a further retrenchment and restriction of the private sector of our economy?

For one who has faith in the voluntary way to obtain production the answer is clear—it is the most useful means available and the means most likely to accomplish, both domestically and internationally, the end result desired by those who make our national policy. Its great characteristics are its flexibility and its capacity to utilize most effectually in production the combined talents of the members of the individual productive groups which are the essence of our voluntary system. In the long run the unhampered voluntary approach has the inherent strength to prevail; only through such means can our national economic objectives as a people be achieved.

A case in point is at hand. With the Iron Curtain countries' avowed intentions to dominate the world through economic-political penetration, our own government, in conjunction with the governments of other free nations, must and can develop its own constructive program.

In this context of a national problem it is only natural for our government to turn to private productive groups, not to formulate our national policy or to dominate its administration but to ask for the invaluable cooperation and contribution of that which the productive groups know best—production itself and all that the word "production" implies.

If that national policy encompasses the encouragement of economic growth in the less developed countries of the world, who better than resourceful private groups can meet the individual economic needs of the extremely varying situations in the respective countries? Private productive groups have done this successfully before and are doing it today. The addition of a national objective does not end their usefulness but rather enhances their opportunities for service.

How to do all this is beyond the scope of our consideration here, but if the national policy objective is to assist the peoples of other lands to meet their physical wants more adequately through their own efforts, then the private sections of our economy are indispensable.

Will there be much which only government can do in the international field? Undoubtedly and properly. But how much greater and more lasting the contribution when private efforts can be stimulated to develop productive facilities in foreign lands, when private American groups can transfer their knowledge of innovation to the people of these lands. The effective cooperation that has been developed between American productive groups and the people of newly developing foreign countries demonstrates the degree to which American participation in foreign development has been mutually advantageous to all people, both in foreign lands and in America.

What form the stimulation of private efforts should take, whether by loans, the minimizing of risk, the protection against foreign governmental disruption, commercial assistance, or otherwise, are matters of great importance. The deferring of tax on income from foreign operations until it is utilized in the United States is an example of a useful incentive worth exploring.

Here, however, we seek only to show that groups of individuals productively oriented can and should be a part of a modern government's resourcefulness in effecting national policy, that within the boundaries of their own private objectives these groups can be most helpful without deviation from these objectives, and that, as citizen men, the individuals who compose corporate groups thus serve the national objective as well as their own.

CITIZEN MAN AND HIS ROLE TOWARD GOVERNMENT

As we have seen, this citizen man in a productive group lives a number of lives, or as some say, he has a plural existence. And it must be apparent by now that individuals who compose corporate groups do not lose their duties and privileges as citizens or their opportunities to exercise those duties and privileges merely because they join a production group we call a corporation.

It should also be clear that an individual member of a corporate group, at whatever rank he may be in the group, frequently is called upon to point out the effects that different types of legislative or tax proposals or similar matters will have on the activities of his own group and of similar groups. To sit quietly by when vital decisions are being made which adversely affect a corporation's activities is in substance to let down the group effort. To speak up will be regarded by some as self-serving, and to the degree to which this serves the group's interest, this is true although no cause for criticism. Nonetheless, I think that no one should take exception when any individual member of a corporate group does speak up in the interests of the group on matters which vitally affect its welfare—for example, on the matter of wage and price controls. In fact, if his place in the corporate group calls for that kind of activity, it is his obligation to speak up. He is only partially serving his function if he fails to perform this activity fairly, judiciously, and appropriately—if he fails to show how his group's function and the objectives of society are interrelated.

It is, of course, not feasible to pursue every matter which may have an effect on the group's affairs. There will be aplenty to do on the public proposals which do have an immediately demonstrable effect on the group's activities.

How any group implements its interest in public affairs is a matter to be tailored to the needs of the group. But of this I am certain: in this area we are, most importantly, dealing with people. It is only natural, therefore, to think of the people in the group, from the lowest-paid employee to the highest, as the focal point of support for proper measures or of opposition to harmful legislative action. To this end, explanation of the effects of particular bills to all employees and encouragement to discuss those bills with their local legislators are entirely appropriate.

But that still leaves the question of what an individual in the group should do with respect to exercising his political rights, certainly a most vital part of the role of him whom we call a citizen man.

Let us begin by recognizing that political organization and activity are essential to the functioning of organized government in a voluntary society. There must be proposals and counterproposals for the conduct of the nation's local and national affairs. Knowledge of these and participation in them are vital to citizenship. The nonpolitical citizen is only half a citizen.

But here we are discussing the policy which a corporate group might have with respect to the individual members of its group engaging in politics.

In advancing this interesting subject, let me say that I think it should be the group's policy not to interfere with political activity but to encourage each of its members, whatever his place in the organization, to exercise his citizenship rights. Included in this exercise of citizenship rights is the need for an active interest in, and financial support of, the political party of his choice. His association with a corporate productive group of his fellow citizens should in no way negate this privilege. The citizenship rights of each member of any voluntary group are the same. Whether the group be a union, a farm organization, a corporation, or anything else has nothing to do with the matter.

It necessarily follows that any effort to require or obligate a member of any group to adopt a particular point of view or give support to a particular party is both beyond the purposes of the group and an infringement of the individual's rights as a citizen. The group as such is not in politics. Its individual members should act according to the dictates of their own feelings and their own points of view if they are going to exercise their proper roles as members of our free society.

But it does not follow that the members of any

group may not make known what they believe to be in the group's interest or where a particular candidate for office stands with respect to the interests of the group. If the point is made that this may unduly influence some other members of the group, the further point can be made, and I think with greater persuasiveness, that since we have a secret ballot and so long as the guiding principles of the group are that it is not in politics as a group and that its members are expected to follow the dictates of their own personal judgments, the possibility of pre-empting that judgment is not great.

I think, moreover, we must understand as clearly as possible when it is that we are acting on behalf of the corporate group and when we are acting as individual citizens, even though the activities which affect the welfare of the group as a whole will naturally have a reaction on the personal views of the individual members of the group. In the final analysis, citizen man has a responsibility as a citizen, which, as noted before, is his first responsibility.

More and more it is becoming apparent that the actions taken by our fellows in government can and do have a profound and far-reaching effect upon members of productive groups and their productive capacities. Are we as members of our respective groups not then obligated to do all we can at least to make clear a point of view with respect to the matters in which we are interested—as I do now?

THE CORPORATE GROUP
AND ITS SOCIAL RESPONSE

Up to now we have been discussing primarily the voluntary groups and their economic functioning. We have done this in terms of production, of the work of groups as innovators and as the primary source of strength and support for the physical world in which we live. At the same time we have seen how the group enhances—and, we believe, avoids stultifying—man's individuality and how it vitalizes his creative and spiritual activities.

Corporate groups must and do maintain a variety of relationships beyond those we have discussed, relationships with groups not normally engaged in commercial production, such as nonprofit associations. These groups exercise a profound influence upon our society and hence indirectly affect the whole climate within which economic affairs are conducted. None of us, for example, is unaware of the effect of general education upon economic life in this country. Nor, for that matter, do we underrate the importance of the physical vigor of our people as a prerequisite to reaching desirable national goals.

Moreover, none of us must forget that there exist always the moral and ethical value systems which make possible the maintenance of useful institutions such as corporate organizations; that we must have a rule of law; and that aesthetic, emotional, and other needs of a people must find healthy and suitable outlet if their culture is to be expressed freely in individualistic terms.

Corporate groups have long assisted noncommercial groups. But until recently there has not been full-scale awareness of the interrelationships between the assistance of productive groups and the national culture. Any group of individuals is a part of its environment. And in the aggregate the majority of American people are associated, in one way or another, with the profit-making groups. Therefore, it is clear that mutuality of interest between the profit-making groups and the nonprofit groups is vitally necessary to the well-being of both.

The individuals in these nonprofit groups also serve and have their motivations. They are deeply involved with the best means of securing changes which genuinely contribute to human progress. For example, those in the universities dedicated to the discovery of knowledge and engaged in the study of the humanities and the physical, biological, and social sciences are seekers after fact and truth wherever it is revealed and wherever it leads them. Their value to society cannot be overestimated; they are in fact the mother lode of nuggets constituting much of our social capital.

These and many other individuals have formed themselves into tens of thousands of voluntary associations for private social welfare, educational, cultural, health, and civic activities. It is estimated that including all levels there are probably no less than one million noncommercial voluntary groups. Their number is in itself significant. As in the case of the productive groups, their magnitude in numbers tends to protect against any undue dominance of direction and makes for the diversity and scope which encourages the most widespread participation.

Our central point is that reasonable support of an appropriate number of these nonprofit groups is both a proper and essential function of a profit-motivated group and performance of that function is happily well advanced. Already the aggregate money flow for such support from all business units is many times the combined cash payments of the larger general welfare foundations such as the Ford, Rockefeller, and Carnegie Foundations.

About 20,000 of these corporate units have increasingly well-defined assistance and support programs. Indeed in some instances combined employer-employee contributions constitute the principal support of certain voluntary efforts.

More than money contribution is involved in, for example, the United States Steel group. Employees at all levels of the organization are encouraged to give of their time and efforts to civic, cultural, and other noncommercial activities, and they respond. Throughout industry, in addition to the innumerable nonmanagement employees, it is estimated that more than one million employees at the supervisory and management levels alone are involved in these activities. And this is natural because all employees are first of all citizens.

When a corporate group makes a contribution to a nonprofit group, the motivation is related to the discovery of the general interest and any direct benefit which the corporate group itself receives is only a by-product result. In the easing of the aches and pains of our over-all community, as well as in the advancement of its hopes and dreams, the members of the production group are giving expression to themselves as individuals and as citizens—they are acting naturally.

There are now several clearly defined areas for which business or business-financed units are making contributions. For example, in the case of United States Steel Foundation's current activities which increasingly reflect sustained and significant participation, there are five major programs: these include (1) social welfare; (2) medicine, hospitals, and health; (3) cultural and community needs; (4) science and technology; (5) aid to education. They are evolving programs—hopefully moving with the times and needs.

1. As you would expect, in social welfare the foundation assists local chests and united funds, the Red Cross, the Salvation Army, the Boy Scouts of America, and various other causes. In extending aid within those national limits which prudence suggests and resources allow, the foundation strives to remedy basic problems, through training and research, rather than endeavoring to cope even in small part with the needs for hundreds of millions of dollars of continuous welfare care.

2. In the area of medicine, hospitals, and health the foundation aids fundamental research in over-

coming mental illness, heart disease, and cancer and assists programs related to occupational illnesses. It has supported integrated medical sciences and physical science research; it encourages training in the field of nursing. It helps finance the construction of hospitals. It has supported medical teaching and training.

3. In the cultural and community area the foundation assists slum clearance projects, seeks to improve citizen participation in community problems, helps the attack on illiteracy and assists in the improvement of vocational skills. The foundation also assists selected art museums and symphony and opera societies and otherwise encourages the cultural aspirations of the American people. For example, one recent major grant was for the Lincoln Center for the Performing Arts in New York City.

4. In the realm of science and new technology the foundation makes grants to assist the growth of both basic and applied human knowledge. It has projects or grant programs in the physical sciences as well as in peacetime nuclear applications, in new studies in spatial, serial, and magnitudinal mathematics, and, most importantly, for research on human behavior—singly and in teamplay. The foundation supports leading scientific bodies of the nation

and some abroad. Lately it has begun assistance to the study of ocean resources, of the earth's crust, and of the polar regions.

5. In the aid-to-education area the foundation provides operating help to virtually every accredited private four-year college in the nation; it has a leadership-institution-aid plan to provide significant assistance to great private universities on a sustained basis; it helps unaccredited colleges secure accreditation; it helps institutions to secure more aid from alumni; it assists colleges to utilize their available resources through better scientific management of them; it seeks to further scholarship and excellence by other grants while encouraging the parallel growth of the humanities and the sciences; it provides graduate-study assistance to outstanding young advanced students; it assists the major educational associations in alerting America to its educational needs and in spreading the base of support; it aids libraries and supports research library centers; and it otherwise forwards the use of better teaching methods. Space does not permit concrete illustrations of many of the developments in which the foundation has been privileged to share but I note in passing that one exclusive United States Steel grant has been credited with a major assist in making

possible the tracking of the first Soviet satellite and perhaps saved the nation months of catching-up time. Another grant, to a young graduate student who otherwise today might be operating his father's shoe store in a rural town, furthered the instrumentation of one of America's first space venturers.

In the field of the humanities, our own foundation has led in the endowment of a Council of the Humanities and thus assists in useful seminars for evaluating humanistic problems associated with our technologically oriented society through the publication of scholarly work and grants for the support of fellowships in philosophy, history, literature, and the social sciences generally.

These foundation programs have been underway only in recent years, but contributions have been made by United States Steel from the very beginning of its corporate life. For example, Judge Gary once boarded a night train and carried a $50,000 check to help rebuild a college destroyed by fire the previous day. Since World War I, United States Steel, in company with others, has assisted in defraying the costs of litigation seeking to keep the Greek Orthodox Church in America free—a contest which, if ultimately lost, might mean a large number of American pulpits would become available for propagation of the Moscow line in the hundreds of centers of this denomination in the United States. In World War II, when Hitler watched the retreat from Dunkirk, and our government was unable to act quickly for legal reasons, United States Steel, at the instigation of the government, joined with other corporate contributors to ship a collection of vital guns and ammunition to England just in time to rearm the then weaponless British troops—thus was citizen man in his corporate group helping to write a page in history.

The renaissance taking place in the city of Pittsburgh is a striking and successful instance of citizen man at work clearing the atmosphere of a city; rebuilding its outmoded areas with self-sustaining and highly appreciated civic projects; developing its medical care, education, music, art, and recreation facilities; remaking the face of the city's skyline; and contributing generally to the well-being of all the Pittsburgh community as well as setting an example for other cities. These civic projects, undertaken with public cooperation, were initiated and are being completed primarily by citizen men, individually and in business groups, who have contributed their leadership and their time and funds to provide a very welcome end result.

Recently United States Steel, in concert with others in the steel industry, with the assistance of the Ford Foundation and the cooperation of the State Department, embarked on a large-scale training program for many hundreds of young Hindustani engineers and administrators. This whole project is in fact a case study in what I have called "the transference of know-how" along with an opportunity for people of another culture to examine ours, under the most favorable conditions of objective and subjective interest.

During the present scholastic year a general welfare foundation and a number of corporations or corporate-financed foundations joined together in a project which operates coast to coast with the largest television audience of its kind on record and the most massive experiment in education ever devised. About 400,000 persons listen daily to "Continental Classroom," an early-bird program in atomic-age physics—now extended to include chemistry—designed to improve the teaching of science in high schools throughout the nation. Many of the nation's teachers are taking this educational course for advanced doctoral credit in nearly 400 participating colleges and universities. Of course, industry will eventually benefit in a better trained work force but the major consequence is that all segments of our society simultaneously benefit. Later programs and improved methods of teaching by TV will, I am confident, come to replace this pioneering experimental project but it has already served to point up new vistas in this medium as an adjunct to teaching and may have considerable long-term values in suggesting ways of alleviating the shortage of teachers as well as improving teaching methods. The shared cost of this project is not high. A chief point too is that such a project was launched quickly, and with relative ease, whereas government-sponsored action necessarily must proceed more slowly and look to certain objectives not necessarily essential to private-sector action.

In 1958, total philanthropies in the United States exceeded $7 billion—less than one-seventh coming from corporate-financed foundations or from other corporate groups directly. There is certainly no problem here of dominance. This one-seventh could be greatly enlarged before reaching in any way the point where it would begin to compare in importance with the problem now at hand in potential Federal exercise of dominance over nonprofit institutions, such as universities and colleges.

Let it be said by those who care to do so that a

production group should stick solely to the work of production; that community affairs, whether international, national, or local, are concerns of individuals and not of corporate groups; that it is somehow inconsistent with the profit motivation to make a contribution to a hospital or a university. That point of view does not seem to me to be either a practical one or one which serves to carry out the natural desires of group membership. Certainly most stockholders and most employees would dislike being members of a group which refused to give a thin dime to the community chest fund. They might not be able to explain why they thought it to be in the interest of the group to make a contribution, but they would be very sure that they felt something needed to be done.

In supporting nonprofit voluntary associations our own group works within limited commitments and resources toward our concept of balanced results. This activity does not detract from the main purpose of our corporate group—the profitable production and distribution of goods and services. On the contrary, we think it enhances that activity.

If what I have indicated about the mutuality of interest between voluntary associations of the profit sectors and of the nonprofit sectors does not lead to ready agreement that contributions are purposefully and positively sanctioned by sound policy, the case for prudent involvement can be shown on still other grounds. Many who criticize our modern corporations claim that by overemphasizing the profit-making motive and by judging everything primarily in terms of whether it works or not, the corporate group tends to debase our culture and undercut efforts to strengthen the individual's value system. I can only reply that these criticisms are, of course, all based on suppositions contrary to the individualism in organizations about which I have been speaking and are contrary to the activities of corporate groups in actual operation such as here described.

When understood, it seems to me that the competitive principle which tends to enhance the individual's growth as well as his productivity, is a sufficient answer to this charge. And the participation in the nonprofit voluntary sectors is further evidence of how the nonprofit and the profit sectors are both equally necessary parts of the same culture.

CONCLUSION

I come to a place for a summary.
Our voluntary way of life has for one of its chief

goals the creation and acceptance of constructive change, the path we have found to great progress. And in the realm of the physical welfare of our people, productive groups of individuals working as corporations are among the chief architects of useful change and of the growth in our society.

Lincoln said, "The legitimate object of government is to do for a community of people whatever they need to have done, but cannot do at all, or cannot so well do, for themselves, in their separate and individual capacities." In the realm of private activity, the indispensable object of working together in groups is to enable individuals to do for themselves what they cannot accomplish alone.

Transformations of all kinds have bestirred our land, from supermarkets to gas transmission lines, from nylon to antibiotics, from computing machines controlling steel operations to stereophonic sound, from a meager sustenance to a life of intriguing abundance—even "affluence" according to one opinion. This constant transformation is in a very real sense our America, and the source of this transformation is America's independent, competitive, creative groups.

In a free society there is no other way than the voluntary corporate way. It is the key to a greater society. Any other way will constitute to a greater or a lesser degree an abandonment of the voluntary way.

But like every intangible possession of mankind, the principles underlying this great productive instrumentality can be and are misunderstood, oddly enough many times by those who stand to benefit by them most. Some who should be encouraging fruitful productivity in their corporate groups sometimes seem the most inclined to place road blocks in the way of their own productiveness.

Granting always the presence of social forces and granting always that forces have meaning and that in our day mass unionization is one of those social forces, it nevertheless does not follow that this particular force, however emotionally powerful it may be, should grow so great or adopt such objectives that the impairment of the competitive principle should ensue, nor does it follow that this force should be permitted to impart stagnation to productive activity.

Nor may this social force of great unions be permitted to displace the functions of those of our fellows under our form of government *to* whom the whole community has given the task of legislating *for* the whole community.

By contrast with labor union power, such economic power as corporate groups do achieve arises out of their economic competency, their unprivileged serving in the market place, and their survival under the discipline of that market place. They have no special sanctions of law to ensure an untouchability; they have only an intergroup rivalry to create the powers and the great responsibilities which go with large production. And the inter-group rivalry serves equally well to counterbalance that power. If it is true to say that the wars in Europe were won at least in part in the mills of Pittsburgh and on the assembly lines of Detroit, it is equally true that those mills and those assembly lines were there to be commanded by the people in war only because the people were voluntarily and competitively served to their satisfaction in time of peace. No economic power safely lodged by the disciplines of competition in the hands of consumers is a power that need be feared.

The voluntary cohesiveness and integrity of the productive group is vital. Without this we diminish for our society the values only competition can supply.

This competitive principle can be lost, and with the losing, we shall lose other values in our free society, not the least of which are the unique disciplines of competition.

Make no mistake. To be free, a society must accept this intergroup self-discipline. It will remain free and thus have the benefits of this discipline only so long as the talents and the energies and the resolution of its people keep it so.

We do no one a service by failing to encompass, as part of our management task, a fuller comprehension of what it is we do and for what we have a major responsibility. That responsibility is not only for improving the techniques needed for greater productivity, but, more importantly, for maintaining the greatest instrumentality free men have yet devised for generating production itself.

Thus we return to our beginning, to our attempt to show how men combine their talents voluntarily and creatively in a free society—an inquiry of transcendent importance for all of us if that free society is to be preserved.